D0515508

*T1-BLJ

A Note from the Editor

You are about to take a journey backward in time. Your means of transportation will be the written word and some glorious photographs. Your journey will take you, decade by decade, through the 20th century . . . our century.

Many of the events described in each issue of *Our Century* magazine are famous. Some have perhaps been forgotten. Many of the people were extraordinary, some merely ordinary, a few certainly evil. But all these events and people have one thing in common: they have made this century a fascinating and momentous one.

All of us who worked on *Our Century* hope you find your journey into the past interesting and educational. And most of all we hope you enjoy these "snapshots in time" as much as we enjoyed recapturing them for you.

Tony Napoli
Editor-in-Chief, *Our Century*

Statistics

	1900	1910
Population of the United States	75.9 million	91.9 million
Number of states in the United States	45	46
Population by race:		
White	66.8 million	81.7 million
Negro	8.8 million	9.8 million
American Indian	237,000	265,683
Asian	124,000	143,688
Population by sex:		
Male	38.8 million	47.3 million
Female	37.1 million	44.6 million
Population per square mile	25.6	30.9
Three leading causes of death	Heart disease	Heart disease
	Influenza & Pneumonia	Tuberculosis
	Tuberculosis	Bright's Disease
Three largest cities in the U.S.	New York	New York
	Chicago	Chicago
	Philadelphia	Philadelphia
Unemployment rate	5%	5.9%
Number of students in elementary schools, high schools, and colleges	17 million	20.2 million
Number of students in government Indian schools	22,124	46,131
Average monthly salary for teachers	$27.00	$62.23
Illiteracy rate	10.7%	7.7%
Number of lynchings	115	74
National debt	$1,107,711,257	$1,023,861,531
Number of horses	13.5 million	20.9 million
Record auto speed	1 mile in 51–4/5 seconds	1 mile in 28–1/2 seconds
Occupations:		
Blacksmiths	227,076	240,519
Physicians & Surgeons	132,225	151,132
Actors	8,392	28,297
Carriage drivers	36,794	35,375
Prices:		
pound of coffee	25¢	5¢
three cakes of soap	20¢	45¢
jar of tooth powder	20¢	15¢
rocking chair	$2.50	$3.75
sheets	45¢	65¢ each
pair of lace curtains	61¢	$2.75 a pair
vaudeville theater tickets	50¢	$1.00

OUR CENTURY

For a free color catalog describing Gareth Stevens's list of high-quality children's books, call 1-800-341-3569 (USA) or 1-800-461-9120 (Canada).

ISBN 0-8368-1032-5

This North American edition published by
Gareth Stevens Publishing
1555 North RiverCenter Drive, Suite 201
Milwaukee, Wisconsin 53212, USA

This edition first published in 1993 by Gareth Stevens, Inc. Originally published in 1989 by Fearon Education, 500 Harbor Boulevard, Belmont, California, 94002, with © 1989 by Fearon Education. End matter © 1993 by Gareth Stevens, Inc.

All rights reserved. No part of this book may be reproduced or used in any form or by any means without permission in writing from Gareth Stevens, Inc.

Printed in the United States of America

1 2 3 4 5 6 7 8 9 98 97 96 95 94 93

All photographs: The Bettmann Archive, with the following exceptions: pp. 5-9: National Archives; pp. 23, 45, 52, 63: UPI/Bettmann Newsphotos. Advertisements on endpapers: W.&J. Sloane furniture: The D'Arcy Collection, University of Illinois at Urbana-Champaign; Ford motor car: The Bettmann Archive.

1900-1910

Gareth Stevens Publishing
MILWAUKEE

Recreation

Americans Work Less, Play More

At the beginning of the century most Americans worked long hours. The 12-hour workday was common. And many people worked seven days a week.

Most men got home just in time for dinner. After dinner they might have an hour or so to read the paper. Then it was time for bed. For many women, the workday and workweek was just as long. Housework filled most of their waking hours.

Over the next several years, however, things began to change. For many men the workday was getting shorter. And the new six-day work-week offered at least one day of rest. Some businesses were even beginning to give workers two-week vacations.

Housewives found their work somewhat easier, too. Women used to spend long hours making clothes for their families. Now factories were starting to turn out ready-made clothes. Shopping took a lot less time than sewing.

Stores were also selling a wider variety of foods. Women no longer had to bake crackers, pies, and cakes. They didn't have to churn butter. They could also buy eggs and vege-tables at the grocery stores. They didn't need to keep chickens or care for their own gardens.

To keep food from spoiling, ice-boxes were available. Women didn't have to buy or gather the food every-day. And the iceman even delivered ice to the home.

Even people who lived far from cities could enjoy timesaving prod-ucts. From the Sears, Roebuck and Company catalog they ordered coffee grinders, ice-cream makers, toasters, and gas-burning stoves. The gas stoves were easier to use than wood burners. And they did away with wood-chopping chores.

Americans spent much of their new-found free time at home. They invited friends over for an evening of singing. If they could afford it, they might have a piano or organ in the parlor.

Outside the home, plays and musical performances were popular. Hundreds of theater companies traveled around the country.

Vaudeville was a popular kind of theater. Vaudeville shows might present a dozen or more acts in one night. There would be jugglers, acrobats, singers, dancers, and comedians. There might also be an act with animals doing tricks.

Comedians like W. C. Fields were very popular. Others didn't make such a hit. The Cherry Sisters performed behind a net. That pro-tected them from rotten fruit thrown by the audience.

Traveling circuses were also big attractions. The Ringling Brothers Circus and Barnum & Bailey's Circus played to big crowds in every city where they put up their tents.

People often visited "trolley parks," at the edge of most cities. These parks were built by streetcar companies. They often had ferris wheels and ponds where you could rent boats. They usually featured vaudeville acts on outdoor stages.

During two-week vacations, people enjoyed the mountains or the beach. Many beaches had amuse-ment parks right on the water.

In the early years of the decade a new form of entertainment caught the public's eye. It was called "moving pictures," or "flickering flicks." Most of the shows were just a few minutes long. They usually were about news or travel. Some showed vaudeville acts.

One moving picture show became very popular. It was called *The Great Train Robbery*. It was 12 minutes long and had 14 scenes. It was like a play, only more realistic.

There was no sound, but printed titles told what was going on.

As the decade ended, Americans found themselves with more leisure time than ever before. And for those people who supplied entertainment and outdoor activities, that was good news indeed. ▪

At the turn of the century, a Sunday crowd enjoys a pleasant day at the Long Beach, California, amusement park.

Employment
Jobs in the Cities Growing Fast

From 1900–1910, farm work continued to provide Americans with more jobs than any other kind of employment. But at the same time cities were growing and nonfarming jobs were increasing fast. As new businesses grew, so did paperwork. And so did the need for office workers. Clerks, bookkeepers, and secretaries were in great demand.

During the decade the first portable typewriters appeared, increasing the need for typists as well.

Factories provided many jobs, too. In 1900, six million people worked in factories. And the number was climbing fast.

Many of the nonfarming jobs were held by immigrants. Most of these foreign-born people settled in cities when they came to the United States. They found work in slaughterhouses and heavy industries, like coal and steel. They also worked in factories and workshops, making clothes. Almost always they were paid less than native-born Americans.

In the big cities, jobs were also opening up for women. In 1900 about 20% of American workers were women. They found traditional women's jobs, such as cooking and making clothes. But they were also moving into businesses.

The new working women were finding jobs as secretaries, salespeople, and telephone operators. The hours were long, with few breaks. Usually they got one 15- or 30-minute break a day. But their pay was good— ten dollars or more a week. That was about twice what they'd made cooking or sewing.

Many men objected to women working. They felt that a woman's place was in the home. An article in *Independent* magazine set forth that idea. "Men want a girl who has not rubbed off the peach blossoms of innocence by exposure to a rough world," the article said. Many single working women quit their jobs once they were married.

The federal government has become a big provider of jobs. Here female workers trim U.S. currency at the Treasury Department in Washington, D.C.

The federal government was a big provider of jobs. By 1910 there were 33,057 government workers in Washington, D.C. The departments of the treasury, interior, commerce, and labor were the biggest employers. The government employer with the fewest workers was the White House. It had only 43 people on its payroll.

Outside Washington, 384,088 people worked in government jobs. The biggest employer was the post office.

During the decade people worked an average of 59 hours a week. The average pay was 22 cents an hour. Many people worked for less. The pay for women was lower than that for men. Children were the lowest paid of all workers.

Dangerous Conditions in the Workplace

About 1.7 million American children worked full time in 1900. Often they made as little as 25 cents a day.

Their jobs were often as hard and as dangerous as those of adults.

Workers continue to complain about conditions in the workplace. Many places are unhealthy, unsafe, and actually dangerous. Many buildings don't have fire escapes. Many people work with dangerous chemicals without protection. Miners work in very bad conditions. They use steam drills that kick up clouds of rock dust. Many die from breathing it into their lungs. The drills are nicknamed "widow makers."

Workers continue to fight for better working conditions. They are trying to organize for better pay and shorter hours. But labor unions have had only modest success so far.

One hope for labor was the passage of a minimum wage law. But in 1905 the Supreme Court ruled against it. The court said it violated the Constitution. There would be no guaranteed wage. The employers would continue to decide what was fair to pay their workers. ∎

Some government jobs provide a little more fresh air. Here a forest ranger in the Wallowa National Forest in Oregon enjoys his surroundings.

Many Arizonans still make their living as hunters and trappers far from any towns or cities.

Moving Toward Statehood

The Arizona Territory: A Study in Contrasts

At night America's big cities are alive with a variety of sights and sounds. Automobiles cough and roar. Trolleys rattle and clang. Telegraph and electrical wires hum overhead. Entertainment seekers rush about; they might be going to the theater or the moving pictures. Perhaps they'd be seeing the Wild West story, *The Great Train Robbery*.

But that's just one side of night life in America.

A night in the Arizona Territory is a different story. There, the only sound might be a coyote's howl. Arizonans don't need *The Great Train Robbery* to thrill them. They get plenty of excitement from the real robbers who still roam there. And the best entertainment is a safe night's sleep.

Arizona does have towns with cars and store-lined streets. But much of the territory is open space.

There are still many people living out in the wilds. Most of them are hunters, trappers, and gold seekers.

The first people who lived in Arizona were Indians. They included Navahos, Hopis, Yumas, and Paiutes. Little by little, white people drove them off the land. Finally the Apache Geronimo was defeated in 1886. For the most part that ended the battles with the Indians.

The settlers still had to worry about outlaws, however. Gangs of rustlers often stole cattle. It was easy for them to escape across the border to Mexico because many ranchers were afraid to go after them there.

In 1901, Governor Nathan Oakes Murphy started the Arizona Rangers. They did a good job of hunting down the outlaws. Some of them had once been outlaws themselves. The Rangers were later used to stop labor disputes in the mines.

Some people thought the Rangers were heroes. But other police agencies were jealous of them. And some political leaders thought the Rangers gave the governor too much power. The Rangers were disbanded in 1909.

Since Arizona is not a state, its governors are chosen by the president. But the people of Arizona want to elect their own governor. And they want statehood.

Some people in Washington, like Senator Albert Beveridge, were opposed. After a visit to Arizona, he called it a "mining camp." He said there weren't enough English-speaking people there to make the territory a state. He wanted to combine Arizona and New Mexico into one big state. Even President Theodore Roosevelt liked the idea.

But most people in Arizona didn't. They didn't think they had much in common with people in New Mexico. Most Arizonans were liberal Democrats. New Mexicans were mostly conservative Republicans.

As the decade ended, it looked as if Arizonans would soon get their wish. Richard Sloan had worked hard to get President Taft elected in 1908. So, Taft made him governor of Arizona. Taft also promised to try to get statehood for Arizona.

And, to the relief of Arizonans, he promised that they would not be joined with New Mexico. ■

Modern life has come to some parts of the Arizona territory. Here four well-dressed gentlemen drive a car down a street in Phoenix.

Women's fashions became simpler. Hemlines of dresses reached only to the tops of shoes or just covered them.

Fashion
Styles Get Simpler

As the century began, a new fashion trend was developing. Clothes were becoming simpler. Before 1900 most women had worn long dresses and skirts. A long cloth train had dragged behind them on the ground.

The newer styles are shorter and simpler. The hems reach only to the shoes or just cover them. Of course women still have to lift their hems when crossing streets or climbing stairs.

But a clear change is coming. Some daring styles even show women's ankles! (The ankles, of course, are well-covered by stockings.)

Women's outer clothes are no longer as frilly as they had been in the 1890s. But the undergarments are still stiff and uncomfortable. The hourglass shape is still popular. And

women still faint when their corset strings are pulled too tight.

Children's dress clothes are also uncomfortable. Even young girls wear corsets. Both boys and girls wear heavy underwear, often made of wool. Many boys wear skirts until they are five or six, while older boys wear jackets and knee pants.

Sailor suits are popular for both boys and girls. These outfits have short pants and blouses. French or English sailor caps are usually worn with them.

During the decade men's styles have changed very little. Men wear jackets and suits for business, and a coat with tails is considered proper dress for formal events. A long "frock" coat is suitable outerwear.

A silk top hat is usually worn for

formal events. For daily use, businessmen wear soft felt hats. Bowlers, with rounded tops and narrow brims, are also popular. Workers usually wear caps, which come in many styles. For summer outings, almost every man wears a straw "boater."

Before the century turned, women usually made their clothes. If they could afford it, they might have used a dressmaker.

With many immigrants pouring into the country during the decade, labor became cheaper. Many factories began to make inexpensive clothes. So more and more women were buying these mass-produced clothes.

Many now buy by mail, ready-made clothes from Sears, Roebuck and Company. The company's 1905 catalog listed 150 different types of shirtwaist blouses.

The corsets still pinch. The wool underwear still itches. But as the decade ends, fashions are getting simpler and more comfortable. ∎

Men's fashions during this decade included high stiff shirt collars, close-fitting vests, three-button suit jackets, and soft felt hats.

The Boxer Rebellion

A Bloody Summer Under the Chinese Sun

For 60 years, foreigners had been interfering in China. The Chinese people became tired of it. As the outsiders gained more and more power, China's anger grew.

Finally, the Chinese could stand it no longer. In the summer of 1900, the country exploded in a bloody uprising.

The uprising was started by a secret society called the *I-ho Ch'uan*. In English this name means "Righteous and Harmonious Fists." The group's members did an exercise that looked like boxing to Westerners. Because of that, the group was known to English speakers as the "Boxers."

Their exercise was meant to prepare the mind and body for combat. As they exercised, the Boxers repeated certain sayings. They felt they were being taken over by spirits. Sometimes they even foamed at the mouth.

A Boxer taken over by spirits was supposed to fight without getting hurt. If he got hurt, it was said that he hadn't trained enough. The group may have seemed odd to some

people. But the Boxers would change China's history. They wanted to get rid of all foreigners. That's what most Chinese wanted, too. The Boxers came along at just the right time.

In the 1800s, China had fought wars against European countries and against Japan. The Chinese had always lost. And after each war, the winners had gained a bit more control over China. ⇨

U.S. soldiers on the Chien-Mien Gate in Peking.

done little to help the area. People were angry with the government. Foreigners were also blamed. Some people said the gods were angry because so many Chinese had become Christians.

The Boxers of Shantung seemed to offer a solution. Their slogan was "Overthrow the Ch'ing; destroy the foreigner." The slogan caught on. Soon many people joined the group.

The government let the movement grow. Eventually, the Boxers dropped their attacks on the government. They directed their efforts toward attacking foreigners. Many Chinese leaders saw the Boxers as a tool for getting rid of the foreigners. One of these leaders was a woman named Tz'u-hsi.

They burned houses, schools, and churches.

Tz'u-hsi was the widow of the former emperor. There was a new emperor now. But Tz'u-hsi didn't like the way he ran the country. With help from some princes, she had him put in jail. Then she killed as many of his followers as she could. She became head of the Chinese government.

During the summer of 1900, there was a lot of trouble in north China. The Boxers went on a rampage. They killed Chinese Christians and foreign missionaries. They also killed any other foreigners they could find. They burned houses, schools, and churches. They wrecked trains.

All the while, Tz'u-hsi did nothing to stop them.

Most of the governors in the different areas of China disagreed with Tz'u-hsi. They thought she was foolish to support the Boxers. But, without waging war against her, there was nothing they could do.

Early in 1900, Tz'u-hsi gave out orders that strongly supported the Boxers. That alarmed foreign diplomats living in Peking. They sent word to the city of Tientsin for help. Many troops from different countries were stationed there.

Allied foreign troops enter the south gate in the city of Tientsin. On the left is a U.S. flag. In the foreground are two Chinese who were killed in the fighting.

Foreigners mined the wealth from China's soil. They opened ports for trade with China. But the Chinese traders always came out second best. The railroads and telegraphs in China were controlled by foreigners. Great Britain, Russia, France, Germany, and Japan all controlled parts of China.

Foreign missionaries had also come there. They converted thousands of Chinese to Christian religions. As a result, the Christian Chinese withdrew their money and support from Chinese society. The missionaries also interfered in local government.

"Destroy the Foreigner"

Shantung, in north China, was the main area of unrest. It had suffered from droughts and from floods. The Ch'ing government of Peking had

By June 3, more than 400 marines arrived in Peking. Most diplomats thought they'd need more troops to hold off the Boxers. On June 9, the diplomats sent another message to Tientsin. They asked British admiral Sir Edward Seymour for more troops.

Seymour answered their call. The next day he himself headed for Peking. With him were 2,000 troops from eight different countries.

Seymour planned to make the 80-mile trip by train. That was a problem. The Boxers had destroyed the tracks in many places. Still, Seymour thought his men could repair them as they went along. Fearfully, the diplomats in Peking waited for Seymour. But he never arrived.

Seymour's plan to travel by train was a failure. It was too easy for the Boxers to attack the train. After seven days, Seymour gave up. His plan had been a bad mistake. He could have marched to Peking in less than seven days.

The Chinese Empress declared war on all foreigners. It was a desperate act.

The Chinese government troops thought the plan was very funny. But the diplomats in Peking didn't. They were very angry. They called Seymour "see-no-more." The day Seymour was supposed to arrive in Peking, antiforeigners struck. They attacked a Japanese diplomat and killed him.

On June 17, Tz'u-hsi heard that the foreigners were making a demand. They wanted her to turn over the government to the young emperor. It was only a rumor. Still, it made Tz'u-hsi very angry.

Diplomats Refuse to Leave

Two days later, she ordered all diplomats to leave Peking. They were to be gone by 4 P.M. the next day. A German diplomat went to discuss the order with the Chinese. He was shot and killed.

The next day, the diplomats ignored the demand. Shortly after 4 P.M., the Boxers attacked. They did so with the support of the government.

On June 21, Tz'u-hsi declared war on all foreigners. It was a desperate act. She had no chance of winning. But years of anger at the foreigners had driven her to it.

Diplomats in Peking gathered in the British compound. With them were guards and other foreigners. There were also about 3,000 Chinese Christians there. And about 3,400 Roman Catholics were trapped in a nearby church. The Boxers tried to set the compound on fire. But their efforts failed. Still, they kept the diplomats trapped inside.

Diplomats in Tientsin were also under attack.

Most of China didn't support Tz'u-hsi. Few governors would send troops to help her. ⇨

Foreign troops attack the city of Tientsin.

Meanwhile, an army made up of troops from eight foreign nations gathered near Tientsin. They defeated the Chinese there. Because of disagreements, they didn't head for Peking until August 4. They arrived there ten days later.

British troops reached the diplomats' homes first. Soon after, Japanese troops rescued the Catholics in the church. The foreigners and Chinese Christians had been trapped for 55 days.

Tz'u-hsi escaped from Peking. Soon the foreigners were in control. For several months, they looted much of China. Both soldiers and civilians took part. The foreign countries might have divided up China. But they couldn't reach an agreement.

At last, 11 countries signed the Boxer Protocol. China was forced to execute several government leaders who'd supported the Boxers. The Chinese also had to pay the foreigners a huge sum of money. It came to more than $333 million.

The Boxer Rebellion had been a disaster for China. It had not gotten rid of the foreigners. It had given them more control than ever. The people of China had been defeated once more. Now they were more bitter toward foreigners than before. ■

Officers of allied armies arrive at the Sacred Gate in Peking. Members of the U.S. infantry form lines on both sides of the arriving forces.

A 63-Year Reign

The End of the Victorian Age

January 22, 1901 was a dark day for the British Empire. The church bells tolled sadly all around the world. Millions of people mourned. Many felt as though they'd lost their mother. Queen Victoria was dead.

For 63 years she had ruled her empire. During this long reign, Britain had controlled lands all over the world. Among them were Egypt, Canada, India, and Australia. Britain had also controlled many islands and ports.

Victoria had ruled over one-fourth of the world.

Victoria had ruled over one-fourth of the world. One-fourth of the world's people had called her their queen.

With Victoria as monarch, Britain was the richest country in the world. From the lands she ruled came materials for Britain's factories. The finished goods were sold back to the people in those lands. Britain was called "the workshop of the world."

English was spoken around the world. Clocks were set by Greenwich, England time. English games and sports were played everywhere. ⇨

Queen Victoria ruled England longer than any other monarch.

Great Britain dominated the world. And Victoria dominated Great Britain. Her reign became known as "the Victorian Age."

Victoria was born in 1819. Her uncle, King William IV, had no children of his own. When he died in 1837, Victoria became queen. She was just 18 years old.

Young as Victoria was, she soon won the respect of her people. She worked hard and cared about her subjects.

In 1840 she married her distant cousin from Germany, Prince Albert. It wasn't love at first sight. Their marriage was arranged by her Uncle Leopold. But it worked out well. She and Albert soon fell in love. During their marriage they had nine children.

When Albert died in 1861, Victoria was heartbroken. For many years she dressed in black. She seldom appeared in public.

As queen, Victoria was served by several wise prime ministers. They included Lord Melborne, Sir Robert Peel, Viscount Palmerston, William Gladstone, and Benjamin Disraeli. They helped her make Britain a rich and powerful country.

More Power to Parliament

During the years of Victoria's rule, Britain underwent many changes. More people got the right to vote. Local government became more democratic. Also, much of the monarch's authority was passed on to Parliament. Great Britain's king or queen would soon be mainly symbolic. Still, Victoria's power was great because she was so respected.

When Victoria died, her son Edward VII became king. Edward's style was very different from his mother's. Queen Victoria had been straight-laced and rather stern. Her son enjoyed a good time. He loved playing cards. He liked to be around beautiful women. And he also enjoyed horse racing. His horses won the English Derby three times.

As a ruler, Edward was active in foreign affairs. He helped improve relations with India and Ireland. He became the first English monarch to visit Russia. And he helped pave the way for better relations with France.

But Edward was not Victoria. After nine years of his rule, Britain had lost power. Germany and France were becoming world leaders. Many of the people Britain ruled wanted self-rule. Britain's great days were fading away. The Victorian Age had passed.

In the spring of 1910, Edward died. His reign had been very brief—just nine years. He had been a popular ruler with his subjects. But Edward's impact on Great Britain was rather small. His short time as England's monarch was completely dwarfed by the giant shadow of the 63-year reign of his mother, Victoria.

∎

Edward VII became king at the age of 59. His reign was very brief.

British troops firing a cannon against the Boer regiments.

In Southern Africa

The Boers Battle the British

No taxation without representation! It was an old cry. The Americans had raised it in 1776. They had to pay taxes to the British, but they weren't allowed to vote. Because of that, they went to war.

That cry was heard again in the 1890s. This time the British were making it. They felt that the Boers in southern Africa were treating them unfairly. The British there were paying taxes, but they weren't allowed to vote.

As it had more than 100 years before, the complaint led to war.

The Boers were Dutch farmers in southern Africa. They lived in two republics: the Orange Free State and Transvaal. They didn't like foreigners—"uitlanders," in their language. And they especially disliked the British.

The British ruled Natal and Cape Colony, territories next to the Boer states. They had ideas that angered the Boers. For example, they let some black Africans vote. In the Boer states, no blacks could vote. ⇨

Thousands of troops of the First Welsh regiment arrive in camp. At one point the British had nearly 500,000 troops fighting against the Dutch.

Many British felt their own government was unfair.

When gold was discovered in Transvaal, in 1886, uitlanders rushed in. Most of them were British. Soon they outnumbered the Boers.

The Boers taxed these foreigners heavily, but wouldn't let them vote. The British uitlanders protested. In 1895 some of them rose up against the Boers. Nothing came of it. But it made relations between the Boers and the British even worse.

The British became worried that the Boers might attack their colonies. They brought troops in from England. The Boers felt the British might invade their republics. They asked the British to send the troops back. When the British refused, the Boers declared war.

The Boers won many battles at first. They had a good army. Their soldiers were well trained and they knew the land well. They took over a lot of British territory. In one week

they defeated three British generals. People in England called it "Black Week."

The British didn't have as many soldiers as the Boers. Also, their generals were old-fashioned. They didn't know how to adjust to the land in southern Africa. They depended on railroads to move their troops. But the trains didn't always go to the important areas.

Finally, the British brought in more soldiers. They also brought in better leaders. One of them was Lord Roberts, who took command of the British troops. Another was his chief-of-staff, Lord Kitchener.

Kitchener set up a system of wagons to move troops and supplies. By not having to use the railroads, the British were able to move about more freely. Slowly the British position became strong. It seemed the tide had turned.

The British began to win battles. They captured Bloemfontein, the capital of the the Orange Free State. Next, Lord Roberts's troops took Pretoria, capital of Transvaal.

Boers Refuse to Give Up

It seemed like the war was nearly over. The Boer army was broken up. Still, many of the scattered troops kept fighting.

The British turned the Orange Free State into a British colony. Lord Roberts put many of the Boers in "camps of refuge." They were supposed to be protected there. In truth, the camps were prisons. The conditions in the camps were terrible. More than 20,000 people in the camps died from diseases. Because of the camps, many Boers continued to fight. Boer leaders like Jan Smuts led raids against the British. The British began to realize that the war was far from over.

By 1901, Lord Kitchener had taken command of the British troops. He began a hard campaign against the Boers. He burned farms and crops. He built forts across the Boer lands. Kitchener hoped to win support from some of the Boers. Many were tired of the war. But Kitchener's methods were so harsh he only made them angrier.

In England, people learned about Kitchener's treatment of the Boers. Many British were troubled. They felt their own government was unfair. They wanted to end the war.

The end of the war came in 1902 with the signing of the Treaty of Vereeniging. The Boers agreed to be loyal to the British king. Though they weren't happy about that part of the treaty, they did win many of their demands.

All the Boer prisoners were freed. After a while they were allowed self-government again. They were not punished for fighting against the British. They were allowed to continue speaking Dutch. And, they were also allowed to keep nonwhites from voting.

After a hard, cruel war, the British hadn't gained much. The Boers had lost many battles, but in the long run, they hadn't truly been defeated. ∎

As a British colony, Canada sent volunteer troops to serve under British command in the fighting against the Boers. Here a Canadian regiment seizes a hill in Transvaal.

After Years of Bad Feelings

Russia and Japan Go to War

On the night of February 8, 1904, the Japanese attacked. The two Russian ships at Port Arthur, China, weren't prepared for action. They sat in the harbor with their lights on. Most of the officers were at a party. The men on watch were taken by surprise.

The eight Japanese ships fired 16 torpedoes. Only three of the torpedoes exploded, but both Russian ships were hit.

After the Japanese ships withdrew, the Russians checked for damage. Neither of their ships were badly hurt. The first effects of the attack were small. But the Russians knew there would be a greater effect. They knew they'd be going to war with Japan.

There had been bad feelings between Russia and Japan for years. The two countries were in a fight for power. They each wanted control over China and Korea.

Russia was a huge country, stretching from Europe to the Pacific. Russian leaders had big plans. One of them was the Trans-Siberian Railroad. It would run from the heart of the country to Vladivostok. That was an important port on the Pacific. The railroad would run through Manchuria in northern China. Russia had

A newspaper cartoon published shortly before the outbreak of war between Russia and Japan. It shows the Japanese challenging the Russian bear.

sent troops to Manchuria during the Boxer Rebellion. After the fighting, the troops had remained there.

Russia also had control over Port Arthur in southern China. Japan had once controlled that port. But Russia and other countries forced Japan out. Then Russia moved in and used it as a navy base. And that angered Japan.

In 1904 thousands of Japanese people were living in Korea. Japan wanted to control Korea's trade and industry. Already, they owned all the railroads there. But Russia was also interested in Korea. It wanted to build a military base there.

Japan was willing to make a deal. It would stay out of Manchuria if Russia stayed out of Korea. Several times the Russians agreed. But later they broke the agreements.

Japan began to prepare for war. First, it made an agreement with Great Britain. Great Britain said that no one should get involved in a Japanese-Russian war. If any country helped Russia, Great Britain would help Japan.

Japan's preparations didn't seem to worry Russia. Russia had an army of a million men. It had no need to fear little Japan.

The Tsar Is Pleased

But Japan was well prepared for war. Early in 1904 the Japanese decided to act. Russia hadn't finished the Trans-Siberian railroad. Western Russia was 5,000 miles from the Pacific. Any supplies and troops from there would have to come by horse.

On February 9, the day after the attack on Port Arthur, Japan declared war on Russia. That act pleased Russia's ruler, Tsar Nicholas II. Nicholas knew that many Russians disliked his government. He thought a big victory over Japan would make him popular.

He was right. The Russian people favored the war. They thought they would gain a quick and easy victory. In schools, Russian children sang songs about punishing Japan. They called the Japanese "little yellow monkeys."

But Russia had problems. Only about one-tenth of its army was in the east. General Kuropatkin was head of Russian troops there. He knew he was outnumbered by the Japanese. When the Trans-Siberian railroad was finished, getting troops would be easy. For now, however, Kuropatkin decided to withdraw from the Japanese.

But Kuropatkin wasn't able to withdraw. The Japanese forced him into a major battle. They fought at the Yalu River, which separated Korea from Manchuria. General Kuroki led the Japanese. He had three times as many men as Kuropatkin did. The Russians were badly beaten. ⇨

In their schools, Russian children sang songs about punishing Japan.

The best restaurant in Port Arthur was wrecked by Japanese shells during the siege. The man eating at the table doesn't seem to mind the damage.

The Germans were secretly carrying coal to the Russian ships.

The Japanese army prepares to charge one of the hills surrounding Port Arthur. The Russians finally surrendered the city in January 1905.

The battle shocked people around the world. An Asian army had beaten a European army! That had never happened before. The victory proved the Japanese could fight. That helped them get loans to continue the war. The United States was among the countries helping Japan.

Russians were very upset by Kuropatkin's defeat. It made the people dislike the government even more. Tsar Nicholas became worried. He feared the people might rise up against him. He decided to keep his best and most loyal soldiers near him. That meant that fewer good soldiers could be sent to help Kuropatkin's troops.

At Port Arthur, the fighting went on. Admiral Togo led the Japanese forces. Admiral Makarov was in charge of the Russian navy. In April, Makarov died when his ship was sunk by a mine. His death was a great loss to the Russians.

The Japanese were on patrol outside Port Arthur harbor when one of their ships hit a mine. The Russians saw the ship go down. They also saw that another Japanese ship was damaged.

It was the right time to attack. But the Russians stayed in the harbor and missed their chance. If they had attacked, they might have ended the war in a day.

In May, Japanese soldiers landed near Port Arthur. The Russian troops blocked their way. They fought a hard battle. The Japanese lost many men.

Russian Troops Trapped

The Russians probably could have held out against the attack. But Stossel, the Russian general, lost his nerve. He pulled his troops back into Port Arthur. The Japanese surrounded them. The Russian troops

The Empress Lends a Hand

The Empress of Japan prepared bandages for the war with Russia. Many people thought these bandages had special powers to heal. They were used many times. The officers used them first, then they were given to other soldiers.

The Japanese army used German methods of fighting. The Japanese navy was modeled after the British. All Japanese felt it was an honor to die for their ruler, the Emperor Meji.

The war was popular in Japan. A man who was in jail for murder gave his savings for the war effort. There were many news stories praising him. He was not pardoned, however.

would be trapped there until the end of the war.

The Russians were now afraid that even their ships would be captured. They decided to leave the Port Arthur harbor. As Admiral Witheft led the ships away, the Japanese attacked.

The Japanese guns didn't work well. But they made two lucky hits on Witheft's ship. It was badly damaged, and Witheft was killed. Admiral Togo now had a chance to destroy the Russian's Port Arthur force. Instead he let the Russians retreat back to the harbor.

Most of Russia's ships were on the other side of Russia, in the Baltic Sea. Tsar Nicholas ordered them to go to Port Arthur. But there was little chance they'd get there in time to do any good. The ships had to travel all the way around Africa. They never stopped once on their trip.

That amazed people around the world. The ships burned coal for power. It seemed impossible they could carry enough coal with them. In fact, they couldn't. The Germans were secretly carrying coal to the Russian ships.

General Togo had missed his chance to wipe out the Russian ships. But the Japanese army finally did the job.

The Russian soldiers were well protected in trenches. And they fought hard. The problem was, General Stossel led them badly. The Japanese attacked wave after wave. Finally they took control of a hill above Port Arthur. From there they could fire on the Russian ships in the harbor. They fired shot after shot. Many of them hit their mark and sank most of the Russian ships.

On January 1, 1905, General Stossel surrendered Port Arthur to the Japanese.

The 100,000 Japanese soldiers at Port Arthur could now fight other battles. With Marshal Oyama in command, they headed north. They were going to fight Kuropatkin's troops.

Kuropatkin now had 250,000 soldiers. But they were far from Russia's best. The Japanese pushed the Russians hard. Finally, Kuropatkin made a stand at Mukden, Manchuria.

The battle lasted two weeks. About 60,000 men on each side died. During the fighting, Kuropatkin made a big mistake. He sent his men in the wrong direction. The Japanese acted fast. They fought harder, overcame the Russians, and took the city of Mukden.

Since Port Arthur had fallen, the Russian ships from the Baltic were ordered to Vladivostok instead. They never got there.

The Japanese learned of the plan. They knew in order to reach Vladivostok the Russian ships had to pass through Tsushima Straits. The Japanese wasted no time. Admiral Togo's ships attacked.   ⇨

The battle of Mukden lasted two weeks. Sixty thousand men on each side died.

In August 1904, much of the Russian fleet tried to escape from the harbor at Port Arthur. But the Japanese sank several Russian ships, forcing the rest to retreat back to the harbor.

The Japanese ships were faster than the Russian ships. They also had better weapons. After a 24-hour battle, almost every Russian ship had been sunk. It was a terrible loss for Russia. The Russian people's anger at the tsar grew even greater.

Finally, U.S. President Theodore Roosevelt stepped in. He suggested that Russia and Japan hold peace talks. Both countries agreed. Japan had hoped for a short war. But the battles had gone on and on. Even though Japan had been successful, the country was running short of money. The tsar wanted the war to end, too. He hoped that peace might quiet the angry Russian people at home.

A Popular Russian Count

The peace talks were held in Portsmouth, New Hampshire. The Japanese arrived full of hope. They thought they would gain much, including a large sum of money. One of the Russians at the talks was Count Witte. He became popular with the American leaders and the American press. During the war, Americans had sided with Japan. Now they had begun to favor Russia. That was largely because of Count Witte.

The Americans urged the Japanese to accept the Russian offer. Russia would give up a lot of territory. They would have to leave Korea, Port Arthur, and southern Manchuria. But they would not have to pay Japan any money.

The Japanese didn't like the terms. But they had no choice. They didn't have the money to keep up the war. And America wouldn't lend them any more. The Japanese were very angry. But they signed the Treaty of Portsmouth on September 5, 1905.

For Tsar Nicholas, peace came too late. Soldiers going home from Manchuria turned against their officers. They took over the Trans-Siberian railroad, and held it for a week.

The tsar's loyal troops from the capital finally stopped the uprising. But that didn't end Nicholas's problems. The Russian people continued to struggle against his unpopular government. ■

U.S. President Theodore Roosevelt (center) played a strong role in settling the Russo-Japanese War. Here, Russian and Japanese representatives are shown at the peace conference in Portsmouth, New Hampshire. On the far left is Russia's Count Witte; second from the right is Japan's Baron Komura.

Russia's "Bloody Sunday"

Workers and Peasants Revolt—Tsar Gives In

The Russian people were on the move. On January 22, 1905, about 200,000 of them took to the streets. They marched through St. Petersburg, capital of the Russian empire. Their destination was the Winter Palace of their ruler, Tsar Nicholas II. Nicholas wasn't looking forward to their arrival. The crowd was in an angry mood.

The marchers were mostly workers. Some of them were on strike from a big factory. Many were women and children.

The leader of the march was the young priest Father George Gapon. He had a written message for the tsar. It had been signed by 135,000 people. And it expressed the feelings of most Russians. ⇨

A Russian painting of street fighting during the 1905 Revolution.

"We have been made beggars," the message began. And it went on to tell of the Russian people's problems. They had to work long hours for very little money. They paid high taxes, but they had no vote. They didn't have free elections.

The message finished with a plea to the tsar. "Do not refuse to help your people. Destroy the wall between yourself and your people."

The marchers carried religious pictures and pictures of the tsar. As they marched, they sang "God Save the Tsar." Like most Russians, they trusted the tsar. They called him "Little Father."

Many people didn't think Nicholas himself had caused their problems. They thought the men around the tsar had told him lies. Once he knew how bad the people's problems were, they felt he would act. If only he would listen to the truth.

But Nicholas wasn't about to listen. He didn't trust his people. In fact, he feared them. The night before the march he had fled the capital and had taken his family with him.

Soldiers Fire Without Warning

Nicholas had left several police chiefs in charge. They didn't trust the people either. As they watched the marchers, they began to worry. They knew the workers were angry. There had been several strikes around the city. The marchers all looked peaceful enough. But there were too many of them. Anything could happen.

The tsar's men decided the marchers must not reach the palace. Police and soldiers stopped the march. They told the people to go home. But the people had come too far to leave now. They stood their ground.

Then, without warning, the soldiers began firing into the crowd. The marchers had no weapons. They were helpless against the soldiers' guns. In minutes, hundreds of men,

---

"We have been made beggars," the message began.

Tsar Nicholas II. His reign became even more unpopular after government troops killed hundreds of marchers on the streets of St. Petersburg.

women, and children lay dead. Some 3,000 more were wounded. When the news spread across Russia, people were shocked. They felt their tsar had betrayed them.

That night, Nicholas wrote about the march in his diary. "Troops had to open fire," he wrote. "There were many killed and wounded. God, how painful and sad!" Then he went on to write about a visit from his mother. Nicholas felt bad about the killings. But for him, they were just a bad part of a normal day.

For the people of Russia, however, it was much more. They came to call that day "Bloody Sunday." The people would remember it with bitterness. It was the day they lost faith in the tsar.

"Bloody Sunday" started what became known as the "1905 Revolution." It wasn't a true revolution. The government wasn't overthrown. But the people began to fight against the tsar. They no longer accepted his complete control. They wanted a voice of their own.

For the tsar, the killings were just a bad part of a normal day.

Soon thousands of people went on strike. Factory workers, servants, and office workers left their jobs. Students dropped out of school. By the end of January, 400,000 people were on strike.

More and more people formed unions. Teachers, doctors, lawyers—they all had their unions. Many of these groups wanted a different government. They wanted the laws written down in a constitution. And they wanted to elect their own leaders. Some groups went even further. The Marxists, for example, wanted to completely overthrow the government.

By fall, the tsar's position was clear. He wouldn't give up any of his power.

Millions on Strike

In late September more strikes were called. In Moscow and St. Petersburg, bakers and printers went on strike. Then the railroad workers followed. Soon workers in the post offices and telegraph offices joined them. Workers from banks and factories struck, too.

More than 2,500,000 people went on strike. The many strikes had become one big strike. Across the country, stores were closed. Offices were shut down. The trains stopped running. This was the 1905 Revolution. The Russian people had found a way to control their own country.

Tsar Nicholas felt helpless. He decided not to use force against the strikers. He noted in his diary that it "would have meant rivers of blood. And we should only have been back where we started."

On October 30, Nicholas signed the "October Manifesto." That statement promised civil rights to the Russian people. Also, it said they could elect a "Duma," a group of leaders. The Duma would have some power over the tsar's law.

Many Russians went wild with joy. They thought they had gotten what they wanted. Their anger had given them power to bring Russia to a halt. Now the anger was gone. So they went back to work.

Tsar Ignores Duma

The tsar had promised the people a Duma. It had seemed he and his men were giving up some power. But they weren't.

Count Witte, one of the tsar's advisers, expressed it well. "I have a constitution in my head," he said. "But in my heart, I spit on it!"

Early in 1906, the first Duma was elected. Most of its members were against the tsar. They made many demands. They wanted an end to the death penalty. They wanted

more power for the Duma. The tsar ignored them. Finally, he dissolved the Duma.

Members of the Duma called on the people to take a stand. They told them to refuse to serve in the army. They told them not to pay their taxes. But it did no good. Most people didn't want another fight with the government. Strong feelings had given power to the people in 1905. But now the feelings had died down. The people were tired of fighting.

"I have a constitution in my head," Count Witte said. "But in my heart, I spit on it."

The members of the second Duma were also against the tsar. They did no better than the first Duma. After four months, the tsar dissolved it as well.

Then Nicholas's men took charge. Prime Minister Peter Stolypin changed the election laws. Now there would be fewer peasants—and more wealthy land owners—in the Duma. When the third Duma was elected, the tsar relaxed. Most of its members were friendly toward him.

In the end, the 1905 Revolution hadn't had much effect. Still, the people had tasted power. It was a taste they would not forget. ∎

McKinley Assassinated; Roosevelt Takes Over

At first President McKinley didn't notice the man in black. The party was crowded. As usual, the president was busy talking with guests. As the man approached him, the president reached out to shake hands.

Then suddenly a gunshot rang out. Everyone froze. The president brought his hand to his chest. "Am I shot?" he asked. Then he fell forward.

The man in black turned to run. But several men reached out to grab him. A few began to beat him with their fists. The president shook his head. "Let no one hurt him," he said.

Then he spoke to his secretary in a whisper. "My wife—" he said. "Be careful how you tell her—oh, be careful."

McKinley was quickly taken to a hospital. The doctors there thought he would live, but they were wrong. The shooting took place in Buffalo, New York, on September 6, 1901. Eight days later, President William McKinley lay dead.

The man who shot McKinley was Leon Czolgosz. He was an anarchist, a person opposed to all governments. He said that he had always wanted to kill a great ruler. He was later executed for killing the president.

When McKinley passed away, Vice-President Theodore Roosevelt became president. He said he would follow McKinley's plans. But that wasn't likely. Roosevelt wasn't the kind to follow anyone else's plans. He had his own plans for leading the nation.

The Nation's New Leader

Roosevelt was born in 1858. When he was a boy, no one thought he would ever lead anything. He was small and weak for his age. He also suffered from asthma. When he was

William McKinley was the third U.S. President to be killed by an assassin.

An artist's painting of President McKinley's assassination at the Pan-American Exposition in Buffalo, New York, on September 6, 1901.

12 years old, his father built him a gym. Young Theodore worked hard to become physically fit. By the end of high school he had become a strong young man.

While attending Harvard University, Roosevelt fell in love with Alice Hathaway Lee. They were married on Roosevelt's 22nd birthday.

Tragically, Roosevelt's wife died after giving birth to their daughter, Alice. That very same day, Roosevelt suffered another tragedy. His mother died of typhoid fever.

To help get over his sadness, Roosevelt bought a cattle ranch. He moved there and tried to lose himself in hard work. He tended cattle, and hunted buffalo and other wild animals. Then in 1886 he married Edith Kermit Carow. She was a good match for him. He often followed her advice.

For a while Roosevelt went to work for the Civil Service Commission. He helped make the civil service system fairer. Then he became head of New York City's police force.

The police in New York had a bad reputation. Many of them took bribes and committed crimes. Roosevelt fought hard to make them honest.

On to Washington

In 1896 Roosevelt helped Republican William McKinley get elected president. McKinley wanted to reward Roosevelt. But he didn't really want him to come to Washington. Roosevelt spoke his own mind, and often made people angry.

The next year, McKinley made Roosevelt Assistant Secretary of the Navy. But he didn't serve long. There was trouble in Cuba, and Roosevelt wanted to get involved.

For a long time, Cuba had been ruled by Spain. Now the Cubans wanted to rule themselves. There was talk of war. Roosevelt and many other Americans wanted to help Cuba. McKinley, though, wanted to avoid a war with Spain. Roosevelt didn't think much of McKinley's stand. He said McKinley had "no more backbone than a chocolate eclair."

In February 1898, the American battleship *Maine* was blown up. It happened in a Cuban harbor, and many Americans blamed the Spanish. Two months later, the United States declared war on Spain.

Roosevelt resigned his job in the Navy Department and quickly organized a group of men to fight in Cuba. He called them the "Rough Riders." On July 1, 1898, they fought near the city of Santiago. Roosevelt led his men on a daring charge up a hill. ⇨

As president, Roosevelt became known as a trust buster.

An Active President

Roosevelt was often sick as a boy. But by working out in a gym he became quite strong. As an adult, he was very active. When he lived and worked on his ranch, he would spend 14–16 hours a day in the saddle. While he was president, he went swimming in the Potomac River during the winter—through chunks of floating ice.

Artists loved to draw cartoons of Roosevelt. Once an artist drew a cartoon of Roosevelt with a bear cub. Soon toy makers were making and selling stuffed toy bears. They became known as "Teddy (short for Theodore) Bears."

That attack helped the American troops win a battle. Newspaper stories made Roosevelt and the Rough Riders famous.

After the war, Roosevelt became governor of New York state. As governor, he approved more taxes for large businesses. That made many enemies for him among business people.

The Youngest President

In 1900, McKinley ran for president again. He picked Roosevelt to run as his vice president. They won the election easily. But less than a year later, McKinley was killed. Roosevelt became the 26th president of the United States. He was 42 years old, and the youngest president in U.S. history.

As president, Roosevelt became known as a "trust buster." The trusts were big companies made up of smaller ones. One of them was the Northern Securities Company. It had been formed by J. P. Morgan and other businessmen.

Roosevelt felt the company was too big and powerful. He thought it acted unfairly, using its huge size to ruin smaller companies. He had the government take the Northern Securities Company to court. As a result the company was broken up.

With Roosevelt as president, the government took 43 such companies to court.

Roosevelt also fought lumber companies to save forest land. He turned 125 million acres of forest into national parks. And he brought water to dry western lands. One of his biggest projects was the Roosevelt Dam in Arizona.

Roosevelt became known for his fairness to workers. In 1902, about 140,000 coal miners went on strike. As winter approached, the country's coal supply was running low. People became worried. Many hospitals and schools wouldn't be able to heat their buildings.

Roosevelt worked to bring the miners and their bosses together for talks. Finally, the strike was settled.

The country had coal once more. And the miners got a pay raise. As Roosevelt said, he helped them get a "square deal."

Roosevelt had a favorite saying, "Speak softly and carry a big stick, you will go far." That meant: talk peacefully, but be ready to use force if necessary.

Once, he feared that European countries wanted to gain power in Latin America. He felt Venezuela and Santo Domingo were in danger. He warned the European countries to stay away. If they didn't, he said, there'd be trouble. The United States would act as a "police power." His words were enough. He didn't have to use a "big stick."

In 1902 Roosevelt began talks with Colombia, which controlled the province of Panama. He wanted to build a canal across Panama from the Atlantic to the Pacific. That would make the U.S. Navy more effective. Its ships would be able to move quickly from one ocean to the other.

During the talks, a plan was agreed on. Roosevelt was pleased. But then some Colombians disagreed. Roosevelt became angry. He went into action. He encouraged people in Panama who wanted to revolt against Colombia. With U.S. support the revolt succeeded. Panama became an independent country. The new government in Panama then agreed to the canal.

A "Square Deal"

In 1904 Roosevelt ran for another term in office. His Democratic opponent, Alton Parker, said Roosevelt had taken too much power.

That didn't bother Roosevelt. He promised the voters a "square deal." And the American people showed Roosevelt how much they liked him. He was reelected by two-and-a-half million votes.

In 1905 Roosevelt helped end the war between Russia and Japan. For his efforts, he won the Nobel Prize for peace. Still, Japan and many Japanese-Americans were angry. They didn't think the war settlement was fair. They grew angrier when San Francisco schools segregated Japanese children.

Roosevelt took action. He convinced San Francisco to end the segregation. And he made agreements with Japan that improved relations with the United States.

While in office, Roosevelt made many enemies. Some were big businessmen. Others were in Congress. Many were members of his own Republican party. They worked against him during his last years in office.

He decided not to run for another term in 1908. He supported William Howard Taft as the person to succeed him. With Roosevelt's backing, Taft easily won the election.

In 1909 Roosevelt left office with many good feelings. He had fought hard and had been very successful as president. He said, "I do not believe that anyone else has ever enjoyed the White House as much as I have." ∎

Roosevelt had a favorite saying . . . "Speak softly and carry a big stick . . ."

At age 42, Theodore Roosevelt was the youngest person ever to become president of the United States.

The Wright Brothers Take Off

New 'Aeroplane' Makes Powered Flight

The boy who had come to watch began to shout. "He's flying! He's flying!"

December 17, 1903 was a bitterly cold day. At least it was on the sandbar near Kitty Hawk, North Carolina. There was ice on the ground. The wind came howling off the ocean at 27 miles an hour.

It was a good day to be inside by a warm fire. But Wilbur and Orville Wright could do their work only outdoors. They needed open air. For two months they'd been trying to test their invention. It was a flying machine that they called an "aeroplane." For those two months they'd had mostly bad weather. And they'd had trouble with the plane's parts.

The day before, Wilbur had tried to fly the plane. It had barely lifted off the ground. Then the engine had stalled. It had stayed aloft for only three seconds.

Now it was Orville's turn. Even though the weather was bad, they decided to try again. Before, they'd taken off from a hill. This time they'd try it on flat land. They'd aim the plane into the wind. That should help lift it into the air. There were four other men at Kitty Hawk to help them. And a boy who had come along to watch.

The two brothers had built the plane in their bicycle shop. It weighed 600 pounds. Its wings were about 40 feet across. They'd designed and built the gasoline engine that powered it. In all, the project had cost them about $1,000.

With the four men's help, the Wrights took the plane from a shed. Then they put it on a special wooden track. It was like a train track, but with one rail. They wired the plane down so it wouldn't take off too soon.

When everything was ready, they made a final check. Then Orville climbed out on the plane's lower wing. He stretched out face down. His legs hung out behind the wing. Wilbur tied a strap around his brother's hips to keep him from falling off.

One of the men made a joke. "All that thing needs is a good coat of feathers to make it fly."

Wilbur started the plane's engine. He yelled over the wind and the engine's roar, "Ready?"

Orville gripped the handles that controlled the plane. "Ready!" he shouted.

He let go of the wire that held the plane down. The plane moved down the track, straight into the wind. Wilbur moved with it, holding a wing to keep the plane balanced. As the plane moved, it began to rise. Higher and higher it went until it was ten feet in the air.

A 12-Second Flight

The boy who had come to watch began to shout. "He's flying! He's flying!"

Moments later, the plane landed gently on the sand. Orville undid the strap and crawled off the wing. "How long was I up?" he asked.

Wilbur checked his stopwatch. "Twelve seconds," he said.

The brothers measured the flight path of the plane. It had flown 120 feet. They figured its speed to be about 30 miles an hour. Other people had glided greater distances, the brothers included. But the Wrights had set different goals for this flight.

They'd done what they set out to do. The plane had raised itself into the air by its own power. It had sailed forward without losing speed. And it had landed at a point as high as the one it started from. No one had ever done this before.

Their accomplishment didn't really surprise them. They'd worked out the plans carefully. They expected their plane to fly.

The brothers flew other flights that day. On one, Wilbur flew 852 feet. The flight lasted 59 seconds. Finally they had to call it quits for the day. A strong wind tipped the plane over. It was too damaged to fly again without major repairs.

The Wright brothers wanted the story about their historic flight to break in a Dayton, Ohio newspaper. Dayton was their hometown. But other newspapers ran the story before the Dayton paper had even learned of it.

Finally, the editor of the Dayton paper heard about the flight. But he never ran the story. As far as he was concerned, it wasn't important enough to print. ■

Orville Wright pilots man's first powered flight as his brother Wilbur looks on.

Earthquake Devastates San Francisco

Fire Races Through City, Thousands of Buildings in Ruin

San Francisco began to shake just before dawn on April 18, 1906.

The first wave of the earthquake hit at 5:12 A.M. It lasted 40 seconds. After a 10-second pause, the second wave hit. It lasted 25 seconds. And that was it. The earthquake had lasted little more than a minute. Yet that was more than enough time to cause enormous damage.

In just 65 seconds, the quake ripped apart brick buildings. It broke wooden houses into splinters. It tore pipes and steel rails from the ground. It twisted and crushed bridges. More than 500 people died. Thousands were left homeless. Property worth millions of dollars was completely destroyed.

Until the earthquake struck, San Francisco had been a booming city. It was the most important American port on the Pacific Ocean. It had grown rich from trading with Asian and other countries.

As San Francisco grew richer, its business leaders had made great plans. New streets were being planned. New buildings were going up all over town. Then came the earthquake. And in a little over a minute beautiful San Francisco was a dusty heap of broken buildings.

Damage was worst where creeks or the bay had been filled in with dirt. The ground there wasn't solid. Many buildings just tipped over, trapping people inside.

In the business district, brick walls crashed into the street. Luckily, most of the buildings were empty at that early hour.

The least damage took place in the hills. That's where many wealthy people lived. Their homes were well built. Many of them rested on rock foundations.

When the quake was over, San Franciscans poured out into the streets. People who were trapped and injured called out for help. But in most places there was only an awful silence. One witness reported that people stood around "like speechless idiots."

The aftershocks started thirteen minutes after the quake. People who had gone back into their homes ran out again. Finally the earth was still. At last, the people relaxed a bit. It looked like the worst of the damage had been done.

Then they noticed the smoke.

San Franciscans had seen bad fires before. More than 50 years earlier a fire had almost destroyed the city. Since then, the city had developed a fine fire-fighting system. It was one of the best in the world.

Even so, some people were worried. One of these was Fire Chief Dennis Sullivan. He felt there wasn't enough water to fight a big fire. But

his men had been doing a good job fighting the most recent blazes. So most people were not alarmed by Sullivan's concerns.

The city might have been prepared for one or two large fires. But San Francisco had never faced a situation like this before.

More than 500 people died in the quake.

At least 50 fires started up all over town. The quake had ripped out electrical wires. It had exploded gas pipes. It had knocked over stoves and gas lamps. And to make matters worse there were no fire alarms. ⇨

San Francisco's Mason Street a little more than an hour after the earthquake struck.

The intersection of Market and Sixth Street lies in ruins after the quake and fire.

The quake had destroyed the city's alarm system.

Fire Hydrants Empty

All across the city, firefighters hitched up their horses. Once in the street, they headed for the nearest cloud of smoke. In most cases it was of no use. When they attached their hoses to fire hydrants, no water came out. The quake had broken most of the city's water pipes.

Without water, there was little the firefighters could do. The blazes spread throughout the city.

The biggest fire was started when a woman tried to cook breakfast. The quake had ruined her

house, but the stove seemed to work. When she lit it, sparks set the broken wall on fire. There were no firefighters nearby, and the fire quickly spread. The woman's attempt to cook breakfast caused people to call this the "Ham-and-Eggs-Fire."

Fire Chief Sullivan was a victim of the quake. He and his wife lived on the third floor of a fire station. When the quake struck, the Sullivans fell through to the first floor. She wasn't hurt badly, but he was. He died three days later.

After the quake, Mayor Eugene Schmitz headed for City Hall. He found that it had been destroyed. He then went to the Hall of Justice and set up headquarters. There he met with the police and began to make plans. First, he ordered that all the city's bars be closed. Next, he organized a group of men called the "Committee of Safety." They would be in charge during the disaster. Schmitz and the Committee had much work ahead of them. Homeless people needed shelter. Injured people needed treatment. Everyone in the city needed food and water.

When news of the quake reached Los Angeles, the people there offered help. They sent a train that arrived the next night. It contained food, medical supplies, doctors, and nurses.

The Army, which had troops stationed at Fort Mason and the Presidio, also helped. Soldiers with rifles patrolled the city. They were ordered to shoot looters and other criminals.

Around the city, people formed their own groups of helpers. They fought fires. They rescued people who were trapped in buildings.

Many homeless people walked the streets carrying everything they owned. They carried dishes, bird cages, rugs, shoes, buckets, or whatever they could save. Many of the homeless went up into the hills. There they sat and watched the city burn.

Wild stories were told . . . one rumor said that Chicago was under water.

The newspaper offices were destroyed, and the telephone system, too. People had no news, except what they heard from each other. Wild stories were told about the quake's effect on the rest of the country. ⇨

San Francisco's City Hall after the quake and fire. All the city's records were destroyed.

Quake Was Felt For Miles Around

The San Francisco earthquake was enormous. It killed people and destroyed property over thousands of square miles. Fifty miles south of San Francisco, the quake turned acres of giant redwood trees into piles of matchsticks. More than a hundred miles north of the city, a ship at sea felt the quake. The boat shook so hard the captain thought it had struck a raft of logs.

Boat owner Thomas Crowley did a lot of business during the fire. One of his customers was Charles Crocker, head of the Crocker Bank. He hired one of Crowley's boats to take heavy bags and boxes out on the bay and keep them there until the city was safe again. Crowley never asked how much money they put on the boat. "I really didn't want to know," he said.

Writer Jack London, a witness to the devastation, was amazed at the people of San Francisco. He wrote that on the second night of the fire, people were calm and quiet, "while the whole city crashed and roared into ruin." He added: "Never in all San Francisco's history were her people so kind and courteous as on this night of terror."

One rumor said that Chicago was underwater. Some people said that Los Angeles had been destroyed. Others claimed that Seattle and Portland had been wiped out by tidal waves.

Without telephones or newspapers, most San Franciscans didn't realize how bad things were at first. But the rest of the world knew. Newspapers around the world carried front-page stories about the quake and fire.

On the afternoon of April 18 the fires still blazed away. To stop them, the police and army used dynamite. They tried to blow up buildings close to the fires. That way the fires would have no place to spread. But the plan didn't work. The men didn't have enough experience using dynamite. The fires raged on.

Rubble and Ash

After three long days most of the fires had burned out. In some places the firefighters had stopped

Most stores were ruined, but business still went on. All a businessman needed was something to sell.

the blazes. In other places there was nothing left to burn.

The city was a wasteland of rubble and ash. Hotels, libraries, jails, theaters, and restaurants were gone. So were 80 churches and 30 schools. The business district was destroyed. And 250,000 homes were lost.

Even before the fires had gone out, help started pouring in from outside the city. Congress voted to send $2.5 million to San Francisco. Money from 14 foreign countries came in. Japan, Canada, China, and France gave the most.

Trains came in from all over the United States. They carried food and other supplies. In one month, 1,800 carloads of supplies arrived. New York City sent $185,000. Los Angeles sent $10,000 and 20 railroad cars loaded with goods.

Children in many parts of the country sent food to San Francisco. They were let out of school to collect it.

The Barnum & Bailey Circus even sent $20,000. The money,

clothes, and food were given out by city officials.

People found what shelter they could. At first, most people camped out in parks. They covered themselves with rugs and blankets. Many people with homes were afraid to go back to them. They thought the quake might strike again. The army set up tent camps around the city for the homeless.

Cleaning up the city was a huge job. People used picks and shovels to get started. They loaded the remains of their city in wagons. Then the horses hauled the loads away.

San Francisco quickly began to rebuild. Most of the city had running water by May. The electricity was restored by early June. There was a big job ahead, but the people were eager to get started.

Three years later, most of the burned area had been rebuilt. About 20,000 buildings had been replaced. The people were proud. Their city was back on its feet. San Francisco would soon be booming once again. ∎

When the fires were finally out, people walked through the streets to see what was left of their city.

William Howard Taft— The Reluctant President

Whatever Taft did, he would do in Roosevelt's shadow.

On inauguration day 1909, the weather in Washington, D.C. was miserable. So was President William Howard Taft. He had just started one of the most important jobs in the world. And he didn't want it.

Politics didn't interest Taft. Ever since he'd graduated from law school he had wanted to be a judge. But his father had been active in the Republican party. He had pushed Taft into politics.

Taft's first political job came in 1882 when he was 25. His father had done favors for President Chester Arthur. To repay him, the president hired young Taft as a tax collector.

One of Taft's first tasks was to fire several workers. They hadn't done anything wrong. But Arthur wanted to give their jobs to his friends. That was the sort of thing Taft hated about politics. Rather than fire the men, he quit his own job.

In 1886, Taft married Helen "Nellie" Herron. She was smart, and she understood politics very well. She, like Taft's father, wanted him to make a career in public office.

Through his father's connec-tions, Taft was appointed to the Cincinnati Superior Court. Soon after that he was made United States Solicitor General. In that job he worked as a lawyer for the government. It was the kind of work he was well suited for. In his first year Taft won 15 out of 18 cases.

Two years later Taft became a federal judge. It was a job he wanted very much. It would give him valuable experience. Someday he hoped to serve on the United States Supreme Court.

In 1901, during President McKinley's term, Taft's legal career was sidetracked. McKinley made him governor of the Philippines, which America then controlled. Taft's wife was well pleased with his new assignment.

Taft worked hard as governor. He improved the Philippine court system. He set up a better system of keeping records. He pushed through laws that improved health conditions. He also built new roads, harbors, and schools.

In 1901 President McKinley was assassinated. Vice-President Theodore Roosevelt took his place.

William Howard Taft. As president, everyone compared him to the man he succeeded—Theodore Roosevelt.

Roosevelt knew what a good job Taft was doing in the Philippines. Before the next election he made Taft his Secretary of War. Taft had made a good name for himself. Roosevelt figured it could help him win the election.

Roosevelt was right. And Taft soon became a valuable person in the president's cabinet. He was very helpful in getting the Panama Canal built. He also helped Roosevelt end the Russo-Japanese war. Roosevelt appreciated Taft's work. He once said that Washington ran smoothly because "Taft was sitting on the lid."

In 1908 Roosevelt decided not to run for reelection. He wanted Taft to succeed him. At first Taft didn't like the idea. He still wanted to be a Supreme Court Justice.

Comparisons to Roosevelt

But Taft's wife and his brother helped change his mind. With Roosevelt's backing Taft won the Republican nomination. His opponent in the election was Democrat William Jennings Bryan. Taft beat him by more than a million votes.

But Taft wasn't happy as president. He knew people compared him to Roosevelt. Roosevelt was a go-getter. Taft was more thoughtful. He admitted he couldn't please people the way Roosevelt had.

"Our ways are different," he said. And nothing could change that.

Taft did try to carry out many of Roosevelt's plans. It wasn't easy. When the Republicans fought among themselves, he couldn't settle the differences. He lost the support of many liberal Republicans. They wanted him to be another Roosevelt. When he couldn't they felt betrayed.

In spite of his problems, Taft had successes as well. One was the Tarriff Board he established. It helped control charges on goods coming into the country. He also helped get a law passed that made campaign expenses public. It said that people running for office had to tell how much money they spent.

Before Taft, Roosevelt had worked against big businesses that tried to eliminate small ones. He took them to court and tried to break up their operations. In eight years he

had won many of those cases. Because of that, he had become famous as a "trust buster."

Taft was fighting big businesses, too. And he was winning cases at four times the rate that Roosevelt had. But no one called him a "trust buster." He didn't have the personality Roosevelt had. He just wasn't colorful.

One of Taft's strong points was getting things organized. He had his department leaders write down how much money they needed. That way, it was easier to keep track of government costs. Thanks to Taft, the country had its first federal budget.

Despite his skills and hard work, Taft felt lacking as president. He could never fill Roosevelt's shoes. As president he had achieved the dream of many. But it was not his dream.

Someday he would put politics behind him. Maybe then he might sit on the Supreme Court. For the present, he would just do his job. But he knew there would be little pleasure in his work. Whatever he did, he would do in Roosevelt's shadow. ■

Ellis Island in New York City was the first stop in America for millions of European immigrants.

A "Promised Land" for Millions of Immigrants

They came from Italy, Russia, and Ireland. They came from Austria-Hungry and Scandinavia. They came to escape injustice, poverty, or disease. They came because they wanted homes and farms of their own.

What country they came from didn't matter. For them, a new life of freedom and opportunity was the important thing. Between 1900 and 1910, nine million immigrants came to the United States.

The newcomers faced many problems when they arrived. Most had to learn a new language. They had to learn new ways. Everything was new.

When 10-year-old Andrew Corsi arrived from Italy, he was shocked. The men in America didn't wear beards, as in his native country. To him, they looked like women. And he thought that New York's skyscrapers were mountains.

In their new land, immigrants often stuck together. Italians, Jews,

Poles, and others often grouped together in neighborhoods. That way they could speak their own language. And they were reminded of home.

Many Americans welcomed the newcomers. Others, though, hated them. The American politician Thomas Watson called them "the scum of creation."

Some Americans were afraid of the immigrants because they seemed so different. In 1907, a group of fearful Americans protested against Asian immigrants.

That led President Theodore Roosevelt to make an agreement with Japan. It was a so-called "gentleman's agreement." The agreement kept Japanese workers from coming to the United States.

Some union leaders didn't like immigrants for another reason. They thought they lowered the pay scale for everyone. Most immigrants would work for low wages. They were happy for any job they could get.

Some people feared that the immigrants were taking jobs from American workers. But actually, immigrants usually took the hard, dirty jobs that no one else wanted. They worked in crowded rooms making clothes. Such places were called "sweatshops." They worked in mines, factories, or slaughterhouses. They worked 12-hour days, six or seven days a week. They were paid the lowest wages. Often they earned less than $12.50 a week.

Some immigrants became so discouraged that they returned to their old countries. In 1908, about 395,000 immigrants went back to where they'd come from.

Most stayed on, however. Life may have been hard, but for the lucky ones America was a dream come true.

So thought Mary Actin, a Russian Jew who'd come to America. She was impressed by the modern inventions and the freedom. America, she said, was "the promised land." ∎

Admiral Robert Peary

First Man to the North Pole

Admiral Peary's telegram to his wife expressed his joy. "Have made good at last," it said. "I have the old pole."

On that day in 1909, Peary had good reason for feeling happy. He was on his way back from an amazing feat. He had traveled farther north than any man before him.

He had just discovered the North Pole.

Robert Peary was born in 1856 in Pennsylvania. At the age of 25 he became a civil engineer for the Navy. After a number of projects, he traveled to Greenland in 1886. His experiences there made him interested in northern lands.

At that time, people thought Greenland was part of North America. As a result of his explorations, Peary proved it was an island.

Between 1893 and 1897 Peary made several trips to the Arctic. He learned a great deal about the frozen north. He wrote about it in his book *Northward over the Great Ice.*

In 1897 he was given a five-year leave from the Navy so he could continue exploring. His goal was to reach the North Pole.

On Peary's first attempt he got within 390 miles of the pole. He was disappointed that he didn't make it all the way. Still, he'd come closer than anyone else.

In 1905 he tried again. His ship, the *Roosevelt,* had been built to sail through masses of floating ice.

He and his men left the ship at Ellesmere Island, near Greenland. With dog sleds, they set out for the pole. The long journey over the ice was full of hardships. At last, Peary and his party had to turn back. They had set another record. They had come within 200 miles of the pole. But Peary was still not satisfied.

Over the next few years Peary made six more trips to the Arctic. In between trips he raised money by giving lectures. Every trip was filled with hardships. Often the men had to turn back because their supplies ran out. On the sixth trip Peary's feet froze.

"It's the pole or bust this time, Mr. President."

In 1908, Peary started out on his final trip. He was 52 years old. President Theodore Roosevelt came to see his ship leave New York. As they were pulling out, Peary's navigator waved to the president. "It's the pole or bust this time, Mr. President," he shouted.

Peary and his men left from Ellesmere Island again. They split up into five groups. Peary took a crew member and four Eskimos with him. The other groups all ran out of supplies and had to turn back. But Peary's group pushed on.

On April 6, 1909, Peary's team reached the North Pole. They marked the spot by planting an American flag there.

When Peary got back to the United States, he got a shock. Another American explorer, Dr. Frederick Cook, claimed that he had reached the pole in 1908.

Peary didn't believe him. Neither did the United States Congress. After checking Cook's story carefully, they decided that he was lying.

For years Peary had worked hard to achieve his goal. At last he accomplished what he'd set out to do. ∎

Admiral Robert Peary

A 1905 assembling plant at the Ford Motor company.

Henry Ford

Automaker Is a Production Genius

The Model T was a success even before it was manufactured.

Henry Ford hated farming. And it was a good thing for America that he did.

Henry Ford was born in Michigan in 1863. His father was a successful farmer. He hoped his son would follow in his footsteps. But the only thing Henry liked about the farm was the machinery. He had other plans for his life.

Ford was a poor student in school. He never learned to read or write very well. But he could fix machines. He could figure out how most of them worked just by looking at them.

When Ford was 16 he left home and went to Detroit. He found work there in a machine shop. He also worked reparing watches. He thought for a while of making watches. But he was more interested in big machinery.

When his father gave him 40 acres of farmland, Ford was

delighted. So was his father. He thought his son was finally coming to his senses. But Ford suprised his father. He moved back to the farm, cleared the land, and built a machine shop on it!

Ford's father couldn't understand his son. He told a friend, "I don't know what will become of him!"

At the time, people were experimenting with gas-powered vehicles. Ford read everything he could find about the new machines.

In 1888, Ford married Clara Bryant and moved to Detroit. Ford went to work as an engineer. But his real interest was in the shed behind his house. There, he was trying to build a car.

Finally he finished it. There was a problem though. The car was too big to fit through the doorway. Ford had to cut a wider doorway with an ax.

The car worked well on a test drive around the block. But Ford continued to improve it. He made two more cars and then went into business.

He wasn't successful at first. But several racing cars he built attracted attention. One of them could go 70 miles an hour!

The Ford Motor Company

Finally, a rich man named Alex Malcomson offered Ford a deal. Malcomson would pay for a company if Ford would make the cars. The business was called the Ford Motor Company.

The first car produced by the Ford Company was the Model A. It was built in 1903. It had an eight-horsepower engine and was started with a crank.

The Ford company turned out many more car models. Most of them sold well. But Ford still had a goal ahead of him. He wanted to make a car that most people could afford. In 1908 he did just that.

The Model T was a success even before it was manufactured. Dealers had more advance orders than they could fill.

Ford made the Model T cheaper by mass-producing it. To do that he set up a special system.

Henry Ford with his son, Edsel, in a Model F Ford car in front of their Detroit, Michigan home.

Ford decided on one design and stuck to it. Each worker in the factory made only one part of the car. The car was built bit by bit by many workers. It was an entirely new system—and it worked.

Ford could now make cars faster than ever. And in business, faster is cheaper.

The Model T was the right car at the right time. Most of the country's roads were dirt. But the model T was well built. It could bounce along those roads without harm. Best of all, it was cheap. In 1909 the Model T sold for $950. That was a price the average worker could afford.

Henry Ford's dream car had become a reality. Now he was ready to put America on the road. ■

The world's first regular factory-produced Model T, 1908.

Marie Curie
First Woman Nobel Prize Winner

Marya Sklodowski graduated from high school with highest honors. The gold medal she won for her work was just a beginning. She would receive a much greater award a quarter of a century later.

Marya was born in Warsaw, Poland, in 1867. When she was 23 she went to Paris, France. There she attended the Sorbonne, a highly regarded university. As she had done in high school, she studied hard. When she got her physics degree, she was ranked first in her class.

Marya married Pierre Curie, a scientist, when she was 28. By then, she was spelling her name in the French style: Marie. Two years after they were married, Marie gave birth to a daughter, Irene.

When Pierre's mother died, his father came to live with them. That worked out well. He looked after Irene while Marie and Pierre worked on projects together.

Many scientists visited the Curie home. One of them was Henri Becquerel. He had discovered that the element uranium gave off strange rays.

Marie was very interested in Becquerel's discovery. She decided she would find out more about the rays. The uranium she worked with was often mixed with the mineral pitchblende. As she experimented she made an amazing discovery. There was something in the pitchblende besides uranium. And it, too, was giving off the rays! Pierre was excited about Marie's discovery. He put aside his own project and began to work with her.

The tests they made showed there were two new elements in the pitchblende. Marie named one of them "polonium," in honor of Poland. The other was named "radium." It was hard work separating the radium from the pitchblende. It took Marie and Pierre four years to find any at all.

Finally, they managed to fill the tip of a teaspoon with radium. For that little amount, they had to use several *tons* of pitchblende!

In 1903 Marie received another honor. She, Pierre, and Becquerel won the Nobel Prize for physics. She had become the first woman ever to win the celebrated award.

Two years later, her joy turned to grief. Pierre was killed in a freak accident. He had slipped while walking in the street. A heavy wagon, pulled by two horses, had run over him. He died instantly.

Marie was heartbroken. Once, she had said she could not live without him. But now she knew she must carry on their work. She took over a teaching job that Pierre had held. She also put together all his writings into a book. And she continued her pioneering work with radium.

She kept Pierre's spirit alive. And her own great spirit never stopped growing. ■

Marie Curie in her laboratory.

Ivan Petrovich Pavlov

Opening Up New Fields of Thought

Scientists are often asked how they get their ideas. Ivan Pavlov could have answered, "A little doggie told me." He would have been telling the truth.

That's just how he developed his theory of conditioned reflexes.

Ivan Petrovich Pavlov was born in Russia in 1849. His father was a parish priest. He himself studied religion before turning to science.

He studied chemistry and physiology at the University of St. Petersburg. From there he went to the Imperial Medical Academy. As a student Pavlov did research on the heart and blood circulation. He was also interested in the digestive system.

Pavlov often worked with animals to learn how they digested their food. He found a way to put a glass window inside a dog's stomach. Then he could actually see the dog's food being digested.

Pavlov used modern methods to keep his laboratory clean. As a result, the animals he studied didn't get infections. One dog with a "window" lived for 14 years.

In 1904 Pavlov received the Nobel Prize for physiology. He was awared the prize for his studies in digestion. As a result of those studies an idea came to him.

Pavlov realized that dogs would salivate, or drool, when they saw food. That was called a "reflex." It was a natural thing to do. The dogs need saliva to help digest the food.

Pavlov tried an experiment. He began to ring a bell every time he showed food to the dogs. At the sight of food, of course, the dogs drooled.

After a while he only rang the bell. He didn't show the dogs the food. But they still drooled. Pavlov knew then that the dogs connected the bell with food.

Drooling when food was in sight was a natural reflex. But drooling at the sound of the bell was a *conditioned* reflex.

The idea seemed simple. But it led to a more exciting idea. If dogs could be "conditioned," what about humans?

Many scientists began to argue about that. They agreed on one thing, though. Pavlov's experiments with dogs had uncovered a new field of thought. ∎

Ivan Pavlov preparing a dog for an experiment in conditioned reflexes.

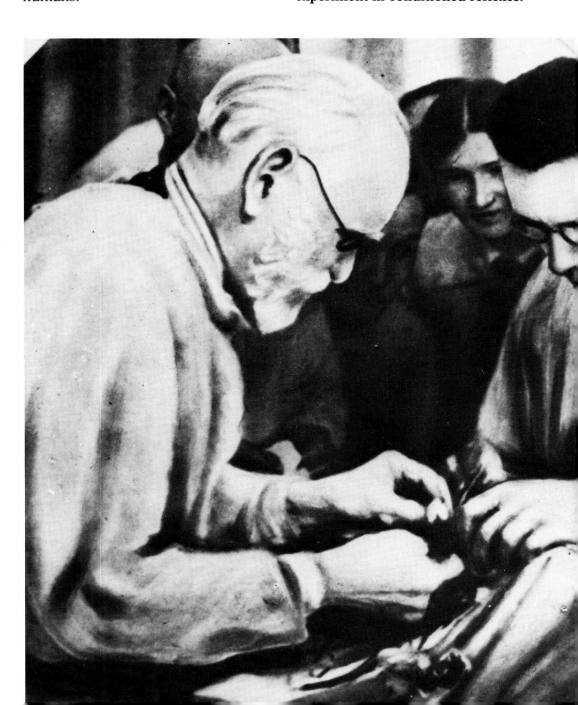

Albert Einstein
From Slow Learner to Physicist

Albert Einstein's work during the decade excited many scientists around the world.

People in Ulm, Germany, felt sorry for the Einstein family. The boy, Albert, seemed so slow to learn. They whispered that there might be something wrong with him. They were wrong. He was just a slow starter.

Albert Einstein was born of Jewish parents in Ulm in 1879. As a young boy, he did poorly in school. He seemed to be a very slow learner. He had difficulty even talking until he was nine years old. Some of his teachers thought he might be retarded.

When Albert was older, his schoolwork improved. But he still had problems with his teachers. Albert was in the habit of asking a lot of questions in class. That bothered his teachers. Most German teachers in those days didn't encourage the students to talk. They wanted them to accept what was taught without question.

To young Einstein, school was like the army, where soldiers did just what they were told. The last thing he wanted to be was a soldier.

Albert began to study quite a lot on his own, outside of school. He had many interests. At one time he was very interested in religion. Later, he talked with a family friend who was studying mathematics. Because Albert showed interest, the friend loaned him some mathematics books. It wasn't long before Einstein knew more about mathematics than his friend.

When Einstein was 15, his family moved to Italy. He stayed behind in Germany to finish school. But he never did. The principal thought he was a bad example for other students. Einstein was told to leave school. That made him very happy.

Einstein joined his family in Italy and lived there a short time. Then his father suggested he go to school in Switzerland. There was a college there he could enter if he passed an exam. Einstein took the exam and failed. But it was clear that he had a great understanding of math.

The head of the college urged him to try again. First, though, he had to go to high school for another year.

Einstein loved Switzerland. He felt much freer there than he had in Germany. In 1894, shortly before his 16th birthday, he became a naturalized Swiss citizen. When he finished the year of high school, he started college.

Einstein became interested in the branch of science called physics. But again he became disappointed with school. Scientists around the world were asking new questions about the universe. At school his teachers weren't interested in such ideas. So just as before, he did most of his learning outside the classroom.

Through a friend, Einstein got a job with the Swiss patent office. There, he examined inventions that people brought to the office. He didn't mind the work, even though the pay was poor. He spent all his spare time thinking about physics.

Einstein had been working on a number of new ideas. In 1905 he wrote about them in a physics magazine. One of the ideas was about the energy of light. Einstein said that it was contained in tiny bundles called *photons*. He also had new ideas about space and time. Some people thought he was a genius. Others thought he was crazy. But his work excited many scientists around the world.

In 1909 Einstein became a professor at the University of Zurich. He was only 30 years old. That wasn't bad for a boy who started out as a slow learner. ∎

Are His Theories Revolutionary or Ridiculous?

Sigmund Freud— The Mind Doctor

Science is on the move, and the public is trying to catch its breath. The Wright brothers' flying machine and Marconi's wireless telegraph signals sent across the ocean are shocking enough. And those are just two of this decade's scientific marvels. What about Robert Koch's breakthrough work on tuberculosis? Madam Curie's discovery of radium? Or Einstein's new theory of relativity? What could come next?

Perhaps the next mystery to be explored will be the inner workings of the human mind. At least that's the goal of a distinguished group of European doctors who visited the United States in 1909. These men are all doctors of the mind, rather than the body. They are all members of the Vienna Psycho-Analytical Association. They were invited by G. Stanley Hall, president of Clark University in Worcester, Massachusetts, to lecture in the United States.

Dr. Sigmund Freud of Vienna is the leader of this controversial group. Now 53, Dr. Freud graduated from the University of Vienna Medical School in 1881. At first he specialized in disorders of the nervous system. Then he went to Paris to study under Dr. Jean-Martin Charcot. There, Freud's work with hypnosis led him to form new ideas about the source and treatment of mental illness.

The basic theory held by Dr. Freud and his followers is that people's behavior is controlled by motives they don't even know about.

He calls this powerful "hidden mind" the *subconscious*. He claims that many illnesses can be treated by working with patients' memories and dreams. He uses the word *psychoanalysis* to describe the discussion process he uses with his patients.

No one denies that Freud is a brilliant man and a great innovator. His many books, beginning with *The Interpretation of Dreams*, published in 1900, have earned him international recognition. Still, his ideas on how the mind works are widely mocked and rejected.

His American audiences, like those in Europe, came away with mixed reactions. Are his theories revolutionary—or just plain ridiculous? Only time will tell. ■

Sigmund Freud (front row, left) brought his radical ideas about how the mind works to the United States in 1909. He and his colleagues came to this country at the invitation of G. Stanley Hall (front row, center) who is the president of Clark University of Worcester, Massachusetts. Others in Freud's party were A. A. Brill, Ernest Jones, and Sandor Ferenczi (top row, left to right) and Carl Jung (front row, right).

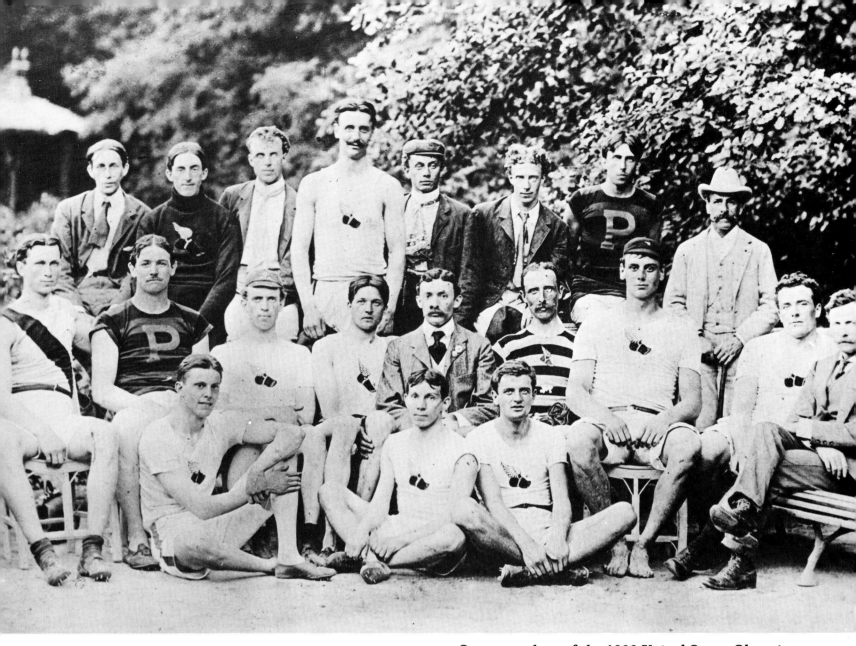

Some members of the 1900 United States Olympic team.

Modern Olympics off to a Rocky Start

Baron Pierre de Coubertin had the right idea. It just took him a while to get his supporters organized.

Coubertin had been the force behind the modern revival of the Olympic Games. Bringing together athletes from around the word was a wonderful idea. Few would argue with that.

But the first modern Games, held in Athens in 1896, were a flop. Organization was poor, and only nine nations attended.

Courbertin and his supporters had higher hopes for the 1900 Games. But, sadly, they were disappointed again.

The 1900 Games were held in Paris. They took place over a five-month period. During that time the Paris Exposition was also being held. It was a huge fair. Most people were more interested in the Exposition than in the Olympics.

As in Athens, the Games again were poorly organized. There were problems when the different events were announced. It wasn't clear that they were part of the Olympics. Some American athletes were really con-

fused. They didn't know they'd been in the Olympics until they won medals. They thought the events were part of the Paris Exposition!

The United States hadn't taken part in the Athens Games. But in 1900, a group of 55 American athletes competed. There was no official team. Several American colleges had sent their best athletes. A few American athletes had entered on their own.

The Games were played on a small field. The track for sprints wasn't level. The jumpers didn't have a soft pit to land in. And the hammer and discus throwers just didn't have enough room. Some of their throws ended up in nearby trees.

In spite of all this, the Americans did well. Alvin Kraenzlein won four gold medals. He took the 60-meter race, high hurdles, low hurdles, and running broad jump. Ray Ewry won three gold medals in various jumping events.

Irving Baxter won a gold medal in the pole vault. That event was on a Sunday and several Americans didn't compete. Later, those who wouldn't compete on Sunday held their own events. One of them vaulted 5¾ inches higher than Baxter had.

Only Eight Countries Compete

The 1904 Games were held in St. Louis, Missouri. Like the Paris Games, they took a back seat to a bigger event. St. Louis was also hosting the World's Fair that year.

And, like the previous two Olympics, the St. Louis Games were poorly organized. Only eight foreign countries took part. Even modern-Olympics-founder Coubertin stayed away.

The most colorful event that year was the marathon. Cars filled with coaches and doctors drove along the course. Runners choked on the dust. Of the 31 men who started, only 14 finished. One runner was chased by a dog.

Felix Carvajal, a mailman from Cuba, had no coach or handler. He arrived in St. Louis with very little money. When he got to the Games, he was poorly dressed for a marathon. He wore heavy shoes, long pants, and a long-sleeved shirt. A helpful American cut Carvajal's shirt and pants down. It made a ragged outfit, but one that was much more suitable for running.

During the marathon, Carvajal talked and joked as he ran. He even stopped at times to talk with spectators. Despite everything, he came in fourth. With the right coaching and clothing he might have won.

American Fred Lorz got the marathon gold medal. But he didn't keep it very long. He later had to turn it over to the second place finisher. It seemed Lorz hadn't won on his own. Along the way he'd gotten a lift from a truck driver!

British Control the Games

The 1908 Olympics were held in London. They were much better organized than the earlier Olympics. But the British had firm control over the events. There were protests about the rules, especially by Americans. But the games went on as planned.

Mel Sheppard was a big winner for the United States. He set an Olympic record for the 1,500-meter race. He topped that with a world record for the 800-meter race.

As in 1904, the 1908 marathon had a strange ending. Dorando Pietri, a candy maker from Italy, seemed a sure winner. He was leading the field with only two miles to go. But when he entered the stadium, he turned the wrong way. Worn out, he staggered, fell, got up, and staggered again.

A few yards from the finish line he fell once more. He was too tired to continue. Finally, track officials lifted him from the ground. They steadied him as he staggered across the finish line ahead of everyone else.

After much talk, the officials reached a decision. Pietri had had too much help. As in 1904, the gold medal went to the second place runner. It was a bitter loss for the Italian team.

When the Games were over, Coubertin and other supporters of the 1908 Games were well pleased. They'd finally put together a successful Olympics. It looked as if the Games would be around for a while.

■

1908 Olympic Games. American Mel Sheppard wins the gold medal in the 1500-meter race. Sheppard also won a gold medal in the 800-meter race.

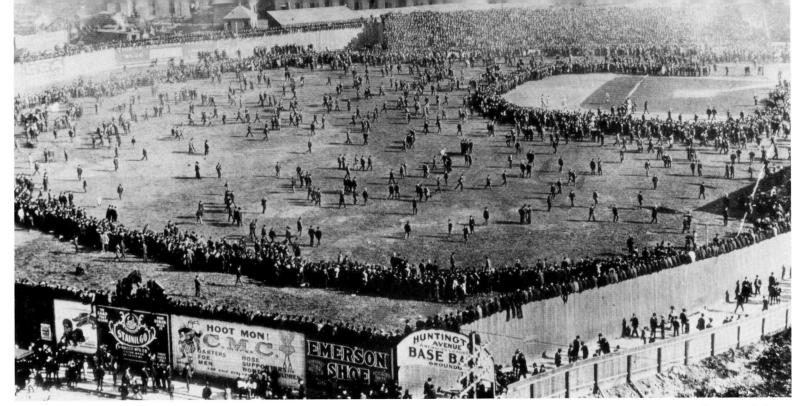

The first World Series featured the American League champion, the Boston Pilgrims, against the National League champion, the Pittsburgh Pirates. Here, fans crowd around the infield at Boston's Huntington Avenue ball field.

Becomes An Annual Event

Baseball Leagues Begin "World Series"

Ever since 1876, baseball's National League had a good thing going. Baseball was as American as apple pie. And for 24 years they had been *the* baseball league in America.

Then, in 1900, sportswriter Byron Bancroft Johnson went and spoiled it. He was the man behind the American League.

At first the leaders of the National League weren't worried. They didn't take the new league seriously.

Soon, though, National League fans began to support the newcomers. National League leaders *did* take *that* seriously. That meant money out of their own pockets.

Something else worried them even more. The American League teams were raiding the National League for talent. By 1903 more than a hundred players had switched leagues. Many of them were crowd-pleasing stars.

Though National League leaders were angry, fans were delighted. As far as they were concerned it meant twice as much baseball.

Finally, the National League

declared a truce. By 1903 it was clear that the American League wasn't going to go away. The question was—how could two leagues survive?

First of all, the player raids had to stop. The two leagues agreed to that. They also made an agreement called "The Joint Playing Rules." These became the official rules of baseball for both leagues.

At the end of the 1903 season a special event was planned. The champions from each league would play a series of games for the world championship. The series would show fans that the two leagues were cooperating. The National League leaders also had other thoughts in mind. They felt their champions would give the American Leaguers a beating.

In that first "World Series," the American League team was the Boston Pilgrims. The National League was represented by the Pittsburgh Pirates. The games would be a best 5-out-of-9 series. To the surprise of the National League leaders, Boston took the series 5–3. Fans of the American League were delighted.

In 1904 Boston won the American League Championship again. The New York Giants won the National League title. But there was no World Series that year.

Series Called Off

Giants manager John McGraw refused to play the Boston team. He called them a "minor league" club. Many people suspected the Giants had other reasons for not playing. They felt McGraw feared that Boston would win again.

In 1905 the World Series was held again. Fans had protested loudly because the 1904 series had been canceled.

This time the leagues agreed to play a 4-out-of-7 series. The Philadelphia Athletics represented the American League. The National League was represented by the New York Giants. This time the Giants were the victors. They took the series easily, 4 games to 1.

McGraw was happy. The fans were happy. And the baseball leagues agreed to make the World Series an annual event. ∎

Christy Mathewson— The Gentleman Hurler

Christy Mathewson

The outstanding baseball pitcher of the decade was an educated, modest gentleman named Christy Mathewson. At Bucknell University, Mathewson was an outstanding athlete in three sports: football, basketball, and baseball. He was also an honor student and class president.

As a star for John McGraw's New York Giants, Mathewson won 263 games over a ten-year period. He led the National League in victories five times and in lowest earned run average three times. Mathewson's finest hour came in the 1905 World Series. Pitching against the American League champion, the Philadelphia Athletics, Mathewson won three games. He allowed the Athletics a total of only 14 hits and shut them out all three times. Mathewson's three victories came within a six-day period. And his last win came after he'd had only one day's rest! This brilliant performance led the Giants to the World Championship and made Mathewson famous to baseball fans everywhere.

Mathewson's success did not go to his head. Through all his triumphs, he remained the same modest, selfless man he was when he first joined the Giants as a 20-year-old college graduate. ■

Ty Cobb— Tough and Talented

Ty Cobb will probably never win a contest as baseball's most popular player. Since joining the Detroit Tigers in 1905, he has earned a reputation as a hard-nosed player with a hair-trigger temper. Over the past few seasons Cobb has had fistfights with umpires, opposing players, fans—and even his own teammates. To say that he is not well liked is to put it mildly.

However, no one who follows baseball can deny one simple fact: Ty Cobb is today's greatest baseball player. Cobb has led the American League in hitting for the last four seasons. He has led the league in runs batted in for three of those four years. It is no coincidence that his team, the Tigers, won the American League pennant in each of those three years.

In addition to his brilliant hitting, Cobb is an excellent base stealer. In fact, he terrorizes opponents on the base paths. By now it's a familiar sight to see Cobb sliding into second or third base with spikes flying.

True, Ty Cobb may not win any popularity contests. But his talent and style of play make him the most feared player in the game. ■

Ty Cobb

In 1910 Jack Johnson retained his heavyweight boxing title by defeating former champ Jim Jeffries in a bout in Reno, Nevada.

Johnson Knocks Out "Great White Hope"

Johnson was the first Negro to win the heavyweight boxing title.

As the decade ended, heavyweight champ Jack Johnson was still amazing—and upsetting—fight fans everywhere. Only two years earlier he had stunned the boxing world. On December 26, 1908, the 30-year-old Johnson had become the first Negro to win the heavyweight boxing crown. The American from Galveston, Texas, had won the title by knocking out Canadian Tommy Burns.

Johnson's victory upset a lot of white people. They didn't like the fact that a Negro now held the heavyweight title. These people searched for a white challenger to take Johnson's title away from him.

Finally in 1910, they convinced former champ Jim Jeffries to come out of retirement. Jeffries agreed to try to regain the title "for the white race." That decision turned out to be a big mistake.

Jeffries hadn't fought in six years. He was out of shape and over-weight. Johnson showed no mercy. He took advantage of every one of Jeffries's weaknesses and pounded him without letup. Finally, in the 15th round, Johnson knocked Jeffries to the ground with a shattering left to the jaw. Johnson had retained his title. He had defeated the "great white hope." ■

Jack London

Author and Adventurer

Best-selling writer Jack London hasn't seen much peace in his life.

He was born John Griffith London in San Francisco, California, in 1876. He grew up in Oakland, across the bay. London's youth was spent on the waterfront. His family was very poor. Much of the time he spent stealing and fighting. When he was 14 he left school. He wanted to escape poverty. And he wanted to find adventure.

For a time, London was an oyster pirate. He sailed about San Francisco Bay in a sailboat. When he could get away with it, he raided other people's oyster beds. At 17 he sailed on a seal-hunting ship in the North Pacific. On that voyage, he visited Japan.

When London returned to America, the country was in a depression. When he couldn't find work, he drifted around the country, sneaking rides in boxcars on trains.

In his travels, London met many other people without jobs. Since he had no work, he decided to educate himself. He began spending much of his time in libraries. One of the writers he read was Karl Marx, the Socialist. Marx's writings influenced London so strongly that he joined the Socialist party.

When London was 19 he decided to go back to school. He studied hard, finished four years of work in one year, and graduated from high school. After high school he

---

London's writings attacked capitalism and defended socialism.

---

attended the University of California at Berkeley. But he quit after a year and joined the gold rush of 1897.

The year before, gold had been discovered in the Klondike region of Canada. London hoped to make a fortune there. He didn't succeed. But he did share some interesting experiences with miners, trappers, and hunters. Later he would write about them.

From Drifter to Best-Selling Author

After a year in the Klondike, London returned to California. He was still poor and without a job. So he decided to try to make a living as a writer. London worked even harder than he had in high school. He wrote jokes, poems, ballads, horror stories, and adventure stories.

In 1900 he published his first book, *Son of the Wolf.* It was a collection of several stories about the Klondike. And it became a best seller. In 1903 London published *Call of the Wild,* an exciting adventure story about a dog in the Klondike. It, too, became a best seller.

In addition to writing books, London also wrote for newspapers. In 1904 he covered the Russo-Japanese War for a newspaper. He was becoming one of the highest paid writers in the country. But he never had much money. He always seemed to spend more than he earned.

In much of his writings London attacked capitalism and defended socialism. He also wrote about the hardships of the poor. His book *The People of the Abyss* was a collection of essays about the poor. His best-known writings were about men and animals. Usually they were fighting to stay alive in a cruel world.

In 1907 London sailed his boat *Snark* halfway around the world. Then in 1909 he published *Martin Eden.* It was about a sailor who became a successful writer. By the end of the book, the man had grown disgusted with people. Martin Eden's life was very much like London's.

That same year London decided to take a break from his travels. He made plans to build a big house in California's Sonoma Valley. There he would create a modern farm. And there, perhaps, he would find some peace. ■

Writer Jack London has also been a sailor and an adventurer.

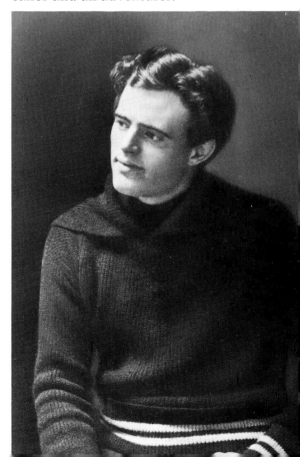

Upton Sinclair

Socialist Muckraker

President Thoedore Roosevelt was disgusted when he read Upton Sinclair's novel, *The Jungle*, in 1906.

That pleased Sinclair. He wasn't trying to tell a pretty story. *The Jungle* was about working in a meat-packing plant. The book told about how hard the people worked, and it described the filthy conditions in the plant.

Later, Roosevelt ordered an investigation of meatpacking plants. When he got the report back he was very angry. He said it was "sickening." Sinclair had told the truth.

In 1906 Roosevelt told Congress to do something about the situation. If they didn't, he said, he would publish the report and embarrass them.

Upton Sinclair: journalist, novelist, and socialist muckraker.

As a result, Congress passed two important laws. One was the Meat Inspection Act. The other was the Federal Food and Drugs Act.

The laws were meant to protect people against impure food. They required that food and drugs be prepared in clean conditions.

Sinclair was pleased that the laws were passed. But he hadn't written *The Jungle* for that purpose. He was more interested in the workers in the plants. He wanted to make their lives better. He wanted the public to feel sympathy for them.

Instead, most of his readers thought about the food they were eating. Sinclair said, "I aimed at the public's heart, and by accident I hit it in the stomach."

Upton Sinclair was born in Baltimore, Maryland, in 1878. He went to college in New York. After college he did advanced study at Columbia Unversity. During that time he supported himself by writing for newspapers.

Politically, he was a Socialist. As a writer, he was a "muckraker." He dug beneath the surface to see what was wrong with society.

Contrast of the Social Class

One of his books was *The Metropolis*. The book tried to show what was wrong with capitalism. Sinclair felt that wealth was divided unfairly. A few people were very rich. But a great many people were poor.

Sinclair said all his books had one theme. That was, "the contrast of the social classes. There are characters from both worlds, the rich and the poor." He said the plots carried his readers from one world to the other.

Many of his books were fiction. But the stories were as filled with facts as any newspaper.

> ## "I aimed at the public's heart and by accident I hit it in the stomach."

The Jungle was Sinclair's sixth book. He got the idea for the story while writing for a socialist newspaper. The paper wanted him to investigate meatpacking plants.

Sinclair did. And he found terrible working conditions there. He was so angry about it, he decided to write *The Jungle*.

The novel told about a family of immigrants from Lithuania. Everyone in the family worked at a meat-packing company. The bad conditions there ruined the health of most of the family. Only the hero, Jurgis Rudkus, survived. He found hope for a better life through the Socialist party.

Since publishing companies found his theme too radical, Sinclair had to publish the book himself. It became a best seller. Sinclair used the money he received from selling it to start a community. It was a co-op. The people in it used a socialistic system of sharing. The building they lived in was Helicon Hall. When it burned down in 1909, the experiment came to an end.

The Metropolis was published in 1908. It was not as popular as *The Jungle* had been, but that didn't stop Sinclair. He continued as a muckraker. And he continued to promote the cause of socialism. ■

Rudyard Kipling
Poet of an Empire

Rudyard Kipling, Nobel Prize winning author. His views on "the white man's burden" were becoming unpopular at the time he was awarded the prize.

The year 1907 should have been a time of joy for Rudyard Kipling. But it wasn't. By then the British writer had published more than 20 books. These included novels, collections of short stories, and books of poetry. Almost all of them were best sellers.

Then in 1907 Kipling was awarded the Nobel Prize for literature. He was the first Englishman ever to win it. Still, he was unhappy.

Kipling loved the British Empire. He expressed that love in most of what he wrote. But, not everyone shared Kipling's feeling of devotion for the British Empire.

Great Britain ruled people all around the world. Many of them lived in India and Africa. Most were dark-skinned.

"The White Man's Burden"

Kipling thought it was Great Britain's duty to protect these people. He called this duty "the white man's burden." The problem was many of these people didn't want Britain's protection. They wanted to be free to govern themselves.

For ten years Kipling had been one of the most successful writers. His books were bought and read by people around the world. Now he was out of step with that world. Small wonder he was unhappy.

Growing Up in England

Kipling was born in Bombay, India, in 1865. His father was in charge of a museum there. When he was young, Indian servants took care of him. He could speak their language, Hindustani, before he could speak English. At the age of five he was sent to school in England. He lived in a foster home and was badly treated. Later, he wrote about that experience in the story "Baa, Baa, Black Sheep."

When Kipling was 17 his parents wanted him to go to college. He said no. He went back to India and became a newspaper writer. In his spare time he wrote poems and short stories.

When he was 22 he published a collection of short stories called *Plain Tales from the Hills*. It soon became a best seller. By the time Kipling returned to England two years later, he was famous. His fame grew when *Barrack-Room Ballads* was published. The book was a collection of poems about British soldiers.

In these poems Kipling told how brave and loyal the soldiers were. Many of the poems were about Private Tommy Atkins. He wasn't an officer, just an ordinary soldier. The book also included "Gunga-Din," which became one of his best-loved poems.

Stories About the Animal World

In 1892 Kipling married Caroline Balestier, an American. For a while they lived in the United States. Kipling didn't get along very well with Americans. He thought they weren't as good as the English. So in 1896, he and his wife moved back to England.

Over the years Kipling has written many stories for children. *The Jungle Book* and *The Second Jungle Book* were big successes. The characters in these books were jungle animals. But their world was much like that of human beings. In the jungle world Kipling created, some animals were leaders, others were teachers. Some were good, and some were evil.

Most of the stories were about Mowgli. He was an Indian boy who had been raised by wolves. As he grew up, he saw he didn't fit into the animal world. In the end, he returned to the world of humans.

One of Kipling's novels takes place in America. *Captains Courageous* is about a teenage boy's adventures on a New England fishing boat.

Perhaps his best-known book is *Kim*. It's a novel about an orphan boy whose parents were Irish. The book gives a colorful picture of life in India. Much of it is based on Kipling's childhood experiences.

During the Boer War of 1899–1902, Kipling went to southern Africa. He became even more convinced that the British Empire should rule there. He still believed it was "the white man's burden." But that idea was becoming unpopular around the world. And sadly for Kipling, so was he. ∎

Isadora Duncan

Dancing Free

Isadora Duncan showed her independence very early in life. Once she complained about the way her ballet lessons were being taught. She thought the positions were ugly and unnatural. She decided to start her own "school" of dance. She even talked other students into following her dance style. At the time, she was only six years old.

She was born in San Francisco, California, in 1878. Her family was poor and she grew used to hardship. When she was 12 she dropped out of school for good. She believed even then that she would one day become a famous dancer.

When Isadora was in her teens she tried to get a dancing job. She went to Augustin Daly who was the director of a famous dance company. Before she danced for him she delivered a speech. "I have discovered the dance" she said. "I have discovered the art which has been lost for 2,000 years."

Whether or not Daly liked her speech, he did like her dancing. He gave her a small part in one of his shows.

Isadora's family felt sure she would become a star. They moved to New York and rented a studio. They were still very poor. So they rented the studio out during the day to make money.

Isadora continued to dance for Daly. The parts were small though, and she made little money. She also often danced in the homes of rich people. They admired her dancing, but they seldom paid her.

When Isadora was 20, she and her family moved to Europe. "America is not ready for what I have to give," she said.

> "America is not ready for what I have to give."

Isadora Duncan has become famous for creating a new freedom in dance.

In Paris, France, in 1900, Isadora "discovered" the dance once more. She also discovered the ancient Greek style of art and dress. Soon, she and her family were wearing Greek costumes. She gave up the stiff uniforms most ballet dancers wore at the time. She began dancing barefoot and wearing loose clothing. She began to create her own style of dance.

Fame in Germany

Isadora worked hard on her dances. Sometimes she stood in front of a full-length mirror for hours. All the while she thought about the dance she was developing.

From Paris, the Duncans moved to Berlin, Germany. There, Isadora found the fame she wanted.

One of her great successes was dancing to the "Blue Danube Waltz." She didn't perform a dance that she'd practiced. Instead, she made up the dance as she went along. And the audiences loved her.

In Berlin, Isadora also started a dancing school for children. She dressed them in the comfortable kind of clothing she wore herself. And she taught them to dance the way she danced. She taught them freedom.

As Isadora's fame spread, she danced constantly. She made a lot of money, but she spent it fast. She loved expensive parties, champagne, and good food.

Most people who saw her were delighted with her dancing. Others, though, found it shocking. Isadora danced in loose-fitting clothes and bare feet. Sometimes she even wore a see-through costume. Some people complained.

But Isadora didn't care what people said. The old ways were not her ways. She believed in her art. She continued to express herself in her dancing and in her life.

Around the world, her message was getting across. She was breathing new life into the art of dance. She had found her own freedom. Now she was teaching other dancers to find a freedom of their own. ∎

Pablo Picasso

Master of Change

"So this is art?" That was a question the people of Paris were asking in 1907.

Pablo Picasso's latest painting was supposed to show five women. But their faces looked like frightening masks. Their arms and legs seemed to be in impossible positions. Many people said they didn't understand it.

For Picasso, that was beside the point. "Everyone wants to understand art," he said. "Why not try to understand the song of a bird?"

To Picasso, works of art were meant to be enjoyed, not talked about. The painting, *The Woman of Avignon,* was done in his newest style. Picasso had developed it with his friend Georges Braque.

One art critic didn't like paintings done in that style. He thought they looked like broken cubes. Soon, people were calling the new style "cubism." Picasso didn't care what they called it. For him it was art.

A Very Young Talent

Picasso was born in Malaga, Spain, in 1881. From his earliest days he loved art. By the age of nine he showed great talent in drawing. By 14 he had already become an excellent painter. He painted in the "realistic" style. The people he painted seemed real and alive.

When Picasso was 23 he moved from Spain to Paris, the center of the art world. Besides paintings, Picasso made beautiful sculptures and drawings. He created with clay, chalk, crayon—anything he could use.

Picasso's artistic style went through several changes. At one time the people in his paintings had long faces. They had sad expressions. There was a feeling of loneliness to

his work. He used a lot of blue tones in the paintings then. That time in his life has been called his "Blue Period."

In 1904 his "Rose Period" began. The paintings had a warmer glow to them. The scenes were more cheerful. His subjects were acrobats and dancers.

The happier mood in Picasso's work may have been because of Fernande Olivier. He met her soon after he came to Paris and they fell in love.

When Picasso began to paint in the cubist style, many people were

upset. They thought he should stay with the more realistic work. They found his new work hard to explain. But that didn't bother him.

"People who try to explain pictures," he said, "are usually barking up the wrong tree."

Picasso let the critics do the talking. He kept on painting. ■

A self-portrait of Pablo Picasso made when the artist was 20 years old.

The Wright Brothers
Pioneers of the Air

When Orville and Wilbur Wright were born, the West was still wild. Pioneers were still heading for the frontier.

By the time they were young men, the frontier had vanished. There didn't seem to be any place left for pioneers.

But the Wright brothers found their own frontier. They just lifted their eyes and saw it waiting for them. The air above would be their new territory.

Wilbur Wright was born in 1867 in Indiana. Orville was born four years later in Ohio. From the time they were very young, the two brothers were interested in machines. As children, they invented and built their own mechanical toys.

When they were in their twenties the brothers invented the "Van Cleve" bicycle. They opened the Wright Cycle Company and built the bikes themselves.

From Bicycles to Gliders

In 1896 they became interested in kites and gliders. The first glider they built measured 16 feet across the wings. It cost them $15 in materials.

The Wrights first flew their glider at Kitty Hawk, North Carolina. Soon they built two more gliders. As they flew them, they learned more and more about flight. They learned how air pressure affected flying. They learned how to solve problems of balance.

They tested many different parts for the gliders. They made more than 200 different kinds of wings. Slowly they were learning how to build a flying machine.

In 1903 they completed one. They called it an "aeroplane." On December 17 of that year, they tried it out. It worked. For the first time, a machine heavier than air had flown. The Wright brothers had crossed into a new frontier. They had opened the skies to aviation.

Their success was not widely noticed. Many before them had tried to fly and failed. Few people believed the plane worked as well as the brothers claimed.

The Wrights offered the plane to the United States government. At first no one took them seriously. Finally, in 1908, the Army said they'd try it out. They'd see if planes could be of any use to them.

Orville showed the Army how the plane flew. He put on several shows for them. On September 17, 1908, he took a passenger, Lieutenant Thomas Selfridge, for a ride. But when the plane was 125 feet in the air, there was trouble. Orville had to make a crash landing. He was badly injured and Selfridge was killed.

Even so, the Army was impressed. They realized that planes were here to stay. So they made a deal to buy planes from the Wright brothers. The two air pioneers had made their point. ∎

Air pioneers Orville (left) and Wilbur Wright.

Triumph Over Handicap

Helen Keller

Helen Keller was the most unusual student at Radcliffe College. By the time she'd graduated, in 1904, she'd already written her life's story.

Titled simply *The Story of My Life*, the book was published in 1902 and became a best seller. That was an amazing accomplishment for such a young person.

Even more amazing was the fact that Helen was deaf and blind.

Helen Keller was born in Alabama in 1882. At birth she was as healthy as most babies. However, at 19 months she became seriously ill. When her illness was over, Helen could neither see nor hear.

For the next five years she was hard to live with. In her book she described herself as a "wild little animal." When she was happy, she laughed. But often she was angry. At those times she'd kick, scratch, and scream.

And then she met Anne Sullivan. Anne was a teacher from Boston's Perkins Institution for the Blind. Anne's childhood had been hard. She'd been badly treated in an orphanage. Because her eyesight was poor, she later went to the Perkins Institution.

After talking with Anne, Helen's parents hired her as a teacher. They hoped she'd be able to help Helen. *They* hadn't had much luck.

Anne moved into the Keller home to be near her student. At first they fought a lot. Helen was spoiled. She'd always had her own way. Anne thought Helen should behave like everyone else. She was firm with the girl, but very kind. In one week they became friends. Helen quickly became well behaved.

Anne taught Helen the alphabet in sign language. But because Helen was blind, she had to feel Anne's hand to know which letter Anne was making. Helen learned many words this way. But she didn't know what they meant.

Then, a month after Anne arrived, something wonderful happened. Anne was "writing" on Helen's hand teaching her the words "mug" and "water." Helen got them mixed up.

Anne took her to a water pump. She held out Helen's hand and began to pump the water. Then she wrote the word "water" on Helen's wet hand. Suddenly Helen understood. "Water" was the name of the cool stuff she had felt. Helen later wrote about that day. She had discovered that "everything had a name."

From then on she loved to learn new words. She said that everything she touched "seemed to quiver with life." She quickly learned the Braille system of reading. The system used raised dots on heavy paper. Blind people could read the special alphabet by touch. Helen learned fast. Soon she was writing poems and stories.

By the time she was ten, Helen could talk with sign language. But she wanted to learn to speak. She worked with a teacher of the deaf. At first, only Anne Sullivan could understand her. But her speech got better. She "listened" to other people by touch. She'd put her fingers on their noses, lips, and throats.

By the age of 16, Helen was able to speak and understand others well. She no longer needed to go to a special school. At her new school all the other students could see and hear.

When Helen's story became well known she began to meet many famous people. She met President Grover Cleveland and the inventor Alexander Graham Bell. The writer Mark Twain became her friend.

Today, Helen travels around the country giving talks. She shows people that severe handicaps can be overcome. Anne Sullivan had touched Helen with her kindness. Now Helen Keller tries to do the same for others. ∎

Helen Keller as a 22-year-old graduate of Radcliffe College.

America's Banker

John Pierpont Morgan

The panic was on! The stock market had been performing poorly in 1907. Many banks were in danger of going out of business. People with money in the banks were worried. They might lose it all. Out of fear, they began to withdraw their funds. That made the panic worse.

Many bankers believed only one man could solve the problem. His name was J. P. Morgan. He was famous for his daring and unusual business deals. He was one of the richest men in the world. And, it turned out, he was just the man to help out the banks.

Morgan quickly got together a group of very wealthy men. He told them they had to loan money to the banks. If they didn't, the banks would go broke. If that happened, they themselves would lose money.

The wealthy men agreed to help. The banks stayed open and the Panic of 1907 passed. The 75-year-old Morgan had done it again.

John Pierpont Morgan was born in Connecticut in 1837. His father, Junius Morgan, was a wealthy banker. Young Morgan went to school in Switzerland and Germany. When he was 19 he went to work at his father's bank.

Morgan learned how to manage money, and how to manage it well. Eventually he formed his own business, J. P. Morgan & Company. His company helped many businesses get started. Often, Morgan would later take control of those businesses. After a business panic in 1893, Morgan became interested in railroads. He helped straighten out several railroad companies that were in financial trouble. Along with some other businessmen, Morgan formed the Northern Securities Company. Through that company he came to control many large railroads.

Later, President Theodore Roosevelt became opposed to the company. He thought it was too large, and it hurt smaller companies by driving them out of business. Finally, in 1904, the government made Morgan break up the company.

Because he was so powerful, Morgan made many enemies. Many people thought he had more power than the government itself. Some people didn't even like the way he looked. Morgan has always been a physically impressive man. He is tall and heavyset. His eyes seem to look right through people. His looks often frightened people.

More Than a Business

Morgan has always had one important business rule. He won't work with anyone he doesn't trust. He has usually been right about his business partners. Most of them have been talented and loyal.

Business hasn't been Morgan's entire life. He is very interested in art. He collects pottery, furniture, statues, paintings, and much more.

Although Morgan is known for being hardheaded in business, he isn't selfish. He has given money to art museums, churches, and hospitals.

Many people have feared his power. Many have hated him for his great wealth. Still, most people have always respected his business sense and his generosity. ■

Banker J. P. Morgan helped prevent a financial panic in 1907.

Prisoner of Sickness

Typhoid Mary

Is it a crime to be sick? That's what Mary Mallon wondered when she was sentenced to prison in 1907. She was known as Typhoid Mary. Her crime wasn't having the disease. Her crime was spreading it.

From 1900 to 1910 typhoid fever was a leading cause of death in the United States. Doctors couldn't do much about it. Still, they knew it was caused by bacteria.

The bacteria, *salmonella typhi*, was passed from one person to another. It was spread by people who had caught typhoid fever. They could pass on the disease through contact with others. Even after they had recovered, they could still be "carrying" the bacteria. Such people were called "carriers." They often spread the bacteria by handling food.

Mary Mallon had come to the United States from Ireland. She was the first person in America to have typhoid fever. She recovered, but she still carried the bacteria. And not only was Mary a carrier—she was also a cook.

There'd been several outbreaks of typhoid fever on Long Island, New York. A health worker named George Soper did some investigating.

Soper traced the disease to Mary. She had been living with a family on Long Island and working as their cook. Several people in the family had typhoid fever. It looked like the chain of disease could be broken. But Mary vanished.

When she was finally found again, she was using a false name. When she was questioned, Mary admitted that she'd cooked for eight different families over a period of several years. Typhoid fever had struck in seven of them. Mary couldn't understand how she could be spreading the disease. After all, she didn't have it herself.

The courts felt they had no choice. Mary was a threat to public health. She was imprisoned in a New York hospital.

Three years later the doctors said she could be released. She was still a carrier. But, if she agreed not to handle people's food she would no longer be a health threat. Mary understood the disease now. She signed a promise that she'd never again work as a cook. And she was warned to keep her promise or she'd face being imprisoned once again. ∎

Mary Mallon was imprisoned in a New York hospital because she was a "carrier" of typhoid.

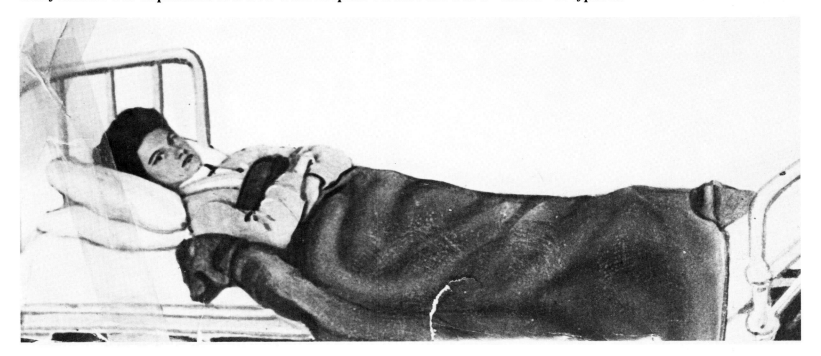

OUR CENTURY: 1900-1910

GLOSSARY

assassination: the murder of a political leader or other important person.

Boers: Dutch farmers who settled in South Africa and fought the British in the Boer War.

Braille: a system of writing with raised dots on paper, invented by Louis Braille, that enables people who are blind to read and write.

cubism: an abstract art movement that began in Paris in the early twentieth century. Cubism involved painting or sculpting the same object or scene from several different angles or perspectives at the same time.

gentleman's agreement: an agreement made verbally, with no written agreement.

the "Great White Hope": a nickname for Jim Jeffries, who tried unsuccessfully to defeat black boxing champion Jack Johnson in 1910.

immigrant: a person who leaves his or her native land to start a new life in another.

Model T: the world's first factory-produced car, made by Henry Ford in 1908.

moving pictures: a term used for silent films, the precursors of today's movies.

muckraker: a journalist who uncovers and publicizes illegal or dangerous activities.

psychoanalysis: a procedure developed by Sigmund Freud which encourages patients to speak freely to a skilled therapist about problems they may be having.

socialism: a political belief that society should not be divided into different classes, and that the wealth of a nation should be shared democratically by all its citizens.

strike: a way of protesting by refusing to work.

Treaty of Vereeniging: the treaty signed in 1902 to end the Boer War. *Vereeniging* means "unity" in the Afrikaaner language spoken by the Boers.

trust: one big company made up of several smaller ones, which often puts smaller companies that don't belong to the trust out of business.

World Series: annual baseball games between the country's two highest-ranked teams. The first World Series game was played in 1903.

BOOKS FOR FURTHER READING

The titles listed below provide more detailed information about some of the people and events described in this book. Ask for them at your local library or bookstore.

Helen Keller. Davidson (Scholastic Inc.)

Pablo Picasso: The Man and the Image. Lyttle (Macmillan Children's Group)

The San Francisco Earthquake. House and Steffens (Lucent Books)

The Theodore Roosevelts. Sandak (Macmillan Children's Group)

The Wright Brothers. Reynolds (Random House)

PLACES TO WRITE OR VISIT

Royal Ontario Museum
100 Queen's Park
Toronto, Ontario M5S 2C6

Museum of Transportation
15 Newton Street
Brookline, MA 02146

The Smithsonian Institution
1000 Jefferson Drive S.W.
Washington, D.C. 20560

INDEX